Little Cities

Catherine Twomey Fosnot
Kimberly Bates
Tammie Hullivan

New Perspectives on Learning, LLC
1194 Ocean Avenue
New London, CT 06320

ISBN-13: 978-1-7335321-4-3

Table of Contents

Unit Overview

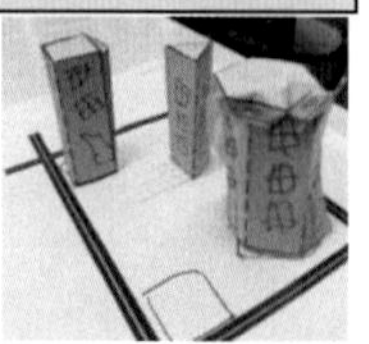

The focus of this unit is the extension of children's early work on navigation and 2-D shapes, developed with the units *Baby's Wild Adventure* and *Shaping Up the Yard,* to the building of 3-D prisms as models for buildings in a miniature city. Within this context, children revisit known 2-D shapes, identifying and drawing triangles, quadrilaterals, and hexagons, and explore how to transform them into 3-D prisms. These models, produced from folding the provided nets, are then glued and placed on maps of city streets. As the unit continues, students discuss how each net has a rectangular surface area that wraps around the sides, and the number of faces of the buildings and their sizes depend on the shape of the polygon base and the lengths of its sides. Next, they make rectangular arrays for tiled patios, determining how many square tiles are needed to cover each area. They discover and prove that the patios have been partitioned fairly into 4 equal areas even though the resulting shapes look different. The unit is designed to align with the CCSS Standards of Practice and the following core objectives:

Geometry 2.G

Reason with shapes and their attributes.

CCSS.MATH.CONTENT.2.G.A.1

Recognize and draw shapes having specified attributes, such as a given number of angles or a given number of equal faces.[1] Identify triangles, quadrilaterals, pentagons, hexagons, and cubes.

CCSS.MATH.CONTENT.2.G.A.2

Partition a rectangle into rows and columns of same-size squares and count to find the total number of them.

CCSS.MATH.CONTENT.2.G.A.3

Partition circles and rectangles into two, three, or four equal shares, describe the shares using the words halves, thirds, half of, a third of, etc., and describe the whole as two halves, three thirds, four fourths. Recognize that equal shares of identical wholes need not have the same shape.

[1] Sizes are compared directly or visually, not compared by measuring.

The unit is also designed as a bridge from the early geometry landscape (Navigation and Shapes) to the later geometry landscape (Area and Perimeter). As such, the landmark big ideas, strategies and models your children will be constructing as they work on the investigations in this unit can be found on the upper part of the landscape of Navigation and Shapes and the lower part of the landscape on area and perimeter. You'll need to use both landscapes for formative assessment as you work with this unit. Both are provided on pages 14 and 15.

The Landscape of Learning

Big Ideas

- Distance and turns are related to lengths and angles of shapes
- Shapes are conserved through flips and rotations
- Shapes are sorted and named according to their properties
- Shapes can be made with other shapes
- One line can represent two bounded areas simultaneously
- 3-D shapes have faces that are 2-D shapes
- Area can be measured by covering and counting non-overlapping units
- A square unit of area in a rectangular array is simultaneously in a row and a column
- Conservation of area
- Equipartitioning of area results in equivalent areas even if the resulting shapes are not congruent

Strategies

- Draws, analyzes, and sorts shapes using Euclidean properties
- Physically rotates objects to prove congruency
- Mentally rotates objects to prove congruency
- Covers a space, but overlaps units or leaves gaps
- Partitioning a shape
- Filling and counting
- Skip-counting
- Repeated addition

Models

- Representing navigation with Euclidean properties of lines and angles
- 2-D shapes
- 3-D shapes
- Grids
- Open Arrays

The Mathematical Landscape

Little Cities is designed to support the further development of the coordination of the two foundational geometries: (1) navigation mapping; and (2) the analysis and recognition of shapes. Current research in cognitive development (Spelke, Lee, and Izard, 2011; Dehaene, Izard, Pica, and Spelke, 2006; Davies and Uttal, 2007) suggests that babies have two core cognitive systems: one that guides them as they move; and another for the analysis of the shapes of small objects for recognition and categorization. But neither system by itself is enough to explain the development of the fundamental Euclidean relationships such as length, angle, and area, which are needed for the deeper understandings of Euclidean geometry. The investigations in this unit involve the transformation of polygons into 3-D prisms and the drawing, matching and sorting of 2-D and 3-D shapes to support the productive coordination of representations from these two core systems.

BIG IDEAS

As young children explore the investigations within the unit, several big ideas arise. These include:

- Distance and turns are related to lengths and angles of shapes
- Shapes are conserved through flips and rotations
- Shapes are sorted and named according to their properties
- Shapes can be made with other shapes
- One line can represent two bounded areas simultaneously
- 3-D shapes have faces that are 2-D shapes
- Area can be measured by covering and counting non-overlapping units
- A square unit of area in a rectangular array is simultaneously in a row and a column
- Conservation of area
- Equipartitioning of area results in equivalent areas even if the resulting shapes are not congruent

Distance and turns are related to angles and lengths of shapes

As children begin to coordinate the representations and characteristics of the two core cognitive systems (mapping the environment and analyzing the characteristics of shapes) they develop a more encompassing way of structuring the information in both. A directional turn becomes understood as an angle (although children most often call it a corner), and distance traveled is understood as a measurable length. Now the two systems are a cohesive whole and a foundation has been built for the later development of area and perimeter of polygons, a measurement of angles as rotations, and eventually the Cartesian-coordinate system–in general, a foundation for the *Euclidean geometry* they will develop in later years.

Shapes are conserved through flips and rotations

Children need many experiences rotating and flipping shapes to ensure they are congruent. In k-1, we often see children who, when shown an isosceles triangle 45 degrees off center, think it is different than the same triangle shown with the base parallel to the edge of the table. By grade 2, we hope to see less confusion around this. But, be alert for this big idea as a few of your children may not yet have developed this idea. Understanding that shapes are conserved through transformation (orientation: flips, rotations, and slides) is a precursor to the development of *transformational geometry*.

Shapes are categorized and named depending on their properties

Early in development, children view figures holistically without analyzing their properties. According to the van Hieles (1985), children at first identify prototypes of basic geometrical figures (triangle, circle, and square). These visual prototypes are then used to identify other similar shapes. A shape is a circle because it looks like a sun; a shape is a rectangle because it looks like a door or a box; and so on. A square often at first seems to be a different sort of shape than a rectangle, and a rhombus does not look like other parallelograms, so these shapes are classified completely separately in the child's mind. If a shape does not sufficiently resemble its prototype, the child may reject the classification. The idea that shapes can be classified and named by their properties (number of sides and angles), in contrast to what they look like, is a huge cognitive leap—one that enables the formation of a larger hierarchical inclusive structure: for example that all 4 sided figures are quadrilaterals, so a rectangle is also a quadrilateral, and a square is the regular version of a rectangle (when all the sides are equal), etc.

Shapes can be made with other shapes

Realizing that different shapes can be combined to make others requires an integration and synthesis of part/whole relations. It is in fact an important precursor to developing the ideas of composing and decomposing areas, which will be needed in grades 3 and up as students engage in constructing area formulas for polygons. To support the development of part/whole relations it is important that children have ample opportunities to build shapes out of other shapes and to represent the relations.

One line can represent two bounded areas simultaneously

Even when children begin to understand that shapes can be decomposed and composed into other shapes, they continue to believe that boundaries cannot be shared. When drawing two adjacent triangles to make a rhombus, for example, you may find your students wanting to draw each line segment of each triangle. Initially this is because they now have a strong understanding of the Euclidean properties of each shape and thus they think it is necessary to represent them (Goodnow, 1977). The idea that one line can simultaneously represent a border between the two triangles (for example using one line across the diameter of the rhombus to represent two triangular areas) is huge and requires some major cognitive reorganization—a big idea for our young mathematicians!

3-D shapes have faces that are 2-D shapes

As children build and explore 3-D shapes, they are often surprised to see that the faces of the shapes are the 2-D shapes they have previously been sorting by properties. This correspondence is important as it fosters the development of an examination of 3-D shapes by their properties. Now the lengths of faces align with the edges of the 3-D shapes and 3-D shapes can be made from nets comprised of polygons!

Area can be measured by covering and counting non-overlapping units

When children engage in determining how many squares fit in the area covering a rectangular array, they need ample opportunities to cover or tile the rectangular space. Just counting the squares on predetermined graph paper does not allow students to develop the idea that one line can represent the shared boundary and the idea that covering an area with squares means edge to edge—gaps and overlapping matter when measuring area.

A square unit of area in a rectangular array is simultaneously in a row and a column

Understanding how arrays are made with aligned rows and columns requires children to think about two dimensions simultaneously (Battista et al. 1998). Every square in a row is also in a column. Notice how children count the tiles. Do they realize that each row is a group and that each row has the same number of squares? This recognition supports the use of skipcounting. Without this cognitive coordination when students attempt to count by ones, they may count across and down, then across the bottom and up the other side. They may count some squares twice because of their lack of understanding how arrays are grids. Coordinating the two dimensions is what will bring students to abandon inefficient counting strategies in favor of skipcounting or repeated addition. Supporting children to draw lines to make grids versus drawing individual squares may help them begin to consider how each square is in a row and a column simultaneously (Outhred and Mitchelmore, 2004). This big idea is a precursor to understanding how L x W can produce a measurement for area.

Conservation of area

Early in the development of an understanding of rectangular shapes and their area, children assume that if shapes look different the areas must be different. They need ample opportunities to consider how a rectangle can be cut in half and the pieces moved without area being gained or lost. For example, a 3x4 rectangle can be cut in half and the halves can be rearranged to form a 6x2 rectangle, but 12 squares are still needed to cover the area.

Equipartitioning of area results in equivalent areas even if the resulting shapes are not congruent

To cut a rectangle into four equivalent sections and understand that the resulting shapes are equivalent even if they are not congruent requires students to have constructed conservation of area. One child may partition a rectangle into 4 equal triangular shapes, while another produces 4 smaller rectangles, but each section is still ¼ of the whole. Be prepared to facilitate rich conversations and justifications on whether these shapes that look quite different have equivalent areas.

STRATEGIES

As you work with the activities in this unit, you will notice that students will use many strategies to solve the problems that are posed to them. Here are some strategies to notice:

- Draws, analyzes, and sorts shapes using Euclidean properties
- Physically rotates objects to prove congruency
- Mentally rotates objects to prove congruency
- Covers a space, but overlaps units or leaves gaps
- Equipartitioning a shape
- Filling and counting
- Skip-counting
- Repeated addition

Draws, analyzes, and sorts shapes using Euclidean properties such as number of sides and angles (often called corners by children)

Early on in development, children often draw polygons as simply closed space. Their triangles are often rounded and not made with three clear straight lines. They also do not sort shapes by their properties, but by what they look like. Squares are not seen as rectangles because they look different. By second grade however, polygons are usually depicted with line segments and angles, rather than simply as bounded curved space, and shapes are sorted into categories by the same properties. All closed shapes with 3 sides and 3 angles, for instance, are sorted and classified as triangles even when they look different.

Physically rotates objects to prove congruency

At first children are not able to determine if the shape would be the same if it was flipped or rotated. They need to physically move the object to check.

Mentally rotates objects to prove congruency

Physical movement of the object to check for congruency is no longer needed. Children are able to mentally rotate or flip to establish congruency.

Covers a space, but overlaps units or leaves gaps

A child may fill a rectangular space with tiles but overlap squares or leave gaps between them. This student may be focusing on just covering the area, rather than on using the tiles to measure the amount of space.

Partitioning a shape

Child draws lines to cut the space into sections equally. They may fold the shape in half and then half again to make fourths and they know when the partitioning is not equal.

Filling and counting

When students do not have a strong understanding of how arrays are comprised of rows and columns–that any given square is part of a row and column simultaneously–the only way they can determine area is to fill the space and count the squares by ones. When students attempt to count by ones, they may count across and down, then across the bottom and up the other side. They may count some squares twice because of their lack of understanding how arrays are grids comprised of equal groups. As you work with students such as these, support them to see how skip-counting by rows or columns is more efficient than counting by ones–but be sure they see where the groups are coming from!

Skip-counting

As students count by ones, the struggle to keep track coupled with the development of the idea that arrays are composed of rows and columns that are each in repeated groups, produces skip-counting. Although students who exhibit this strategy are still structuring additively rather than multiplicatively, it is an advance from counting by ones because they are now grouping.

Repeated addition

Repeated addition is another example of structuring the task additively. Precisely because skip-counting can be difficult, you may find students writing down the number in each row, and then adding repeatedly. This adding is also cumbersome, however, and students may regroup the groups to add more efficiently. This regrouping is an important strategy that is a precursor to the emergence of partial products and doubling and halving.

MATHEMATICAL MODELING

Initially models grow out of representing a situation (Gravemeijer, 1999). In this unit children engage in using shapes as building footprints. They also engage in using provided nets comprised of polygons to form 3-D prisms for models of buildings. As the unit progresses, students use square tiles and grid paper to make rectangular areas for tiled patios and other areas. This unit attempts to foster coordination between the forms of representing the drawings and building of 2-D and 3-D shapes to build a foundation for the development of Euclidean geometry, which demands an understanding and coordination of the attributes of length, distance, angle, and direction.

2-D shapes

The unit is designed to encourage children to represent, sort, classify, and name 2-D shapes (on a plane) by representing them by their Euclidean properties (such as the number of sides and angles).

3-D shapes

The faces of the 3-D shapes are 2-D polygons. As children explore 3-D shapes in this unit, the properties of the 2-D polygons (sides, corners) as well as edges and vertices are used to describe, sort, and discuss relationships.

Grids

Grids are provided in the unit to support students to draw rectangular arrays and to count the squares that cover the space.

Open Arrays

Open arrays are used to represent the partitioning of rectangular patios.

One of the primary thrusts of this unit is to introduce the rectangular array model. The array is a powerful model for multiplicative and geometric thinking because it can support the development of the following:

- a wide range of strategies (counting by ones, skip-counting, repeated addition, doubling, doubling and halving, partial products) and eventually big ideas like the distributive, associative, and commutative properties of multiplication
- visual representations of area and perimeter

The formal development of area is not a goal of this unit, but by the end of second grade multiplication is usually being introduced. Students do not automatically understand the mathematics inherent in the array, and for the array to become a tool for thinking it should be progressively developed in three stages (Gravemeijer 1999):

- ***model of the situation***
- ***model of students' strategies***
- ***model as a tool for thinking***

Model of the situation

Models initially grow out of visual representations of a realistic situation. In this unit, the grid is used to represent the space covered inside rectangular shapes with opportunities presented for students to compose and decompose these shapes. It is important that students also be provided with opportunities to draw and defend their solutions. Number lines can be used for length and width measurements, with lines drawn from points to make rows and columns—gridded areas. Graph paper (also a grid) is used as the medium for cutouts of patios for the buildings in the cities and students explore and keep a record of how many tiles are needed for each patio.

Model of students' strategies

Students benefit from seeing the teacher model their strategies. Once a model has been introduced as a representation of the situation, you can use it to display student strategies during minilessons focused on computation. Towards the end of this unit, the open array is used to model students' early multiplication strategies. If a student says in calculating the number of tiles for a 4 x 12 patio, "I doubled and halved. I substituted 8 x 6," you might draw the following:

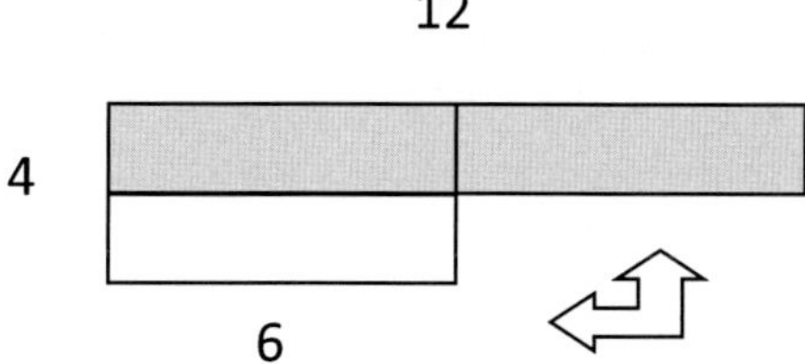

Using representations like these as you do minilessons focused on computation will give students a chance to discuss a variety of strategies they may find useful as they work on the investigations, and it will continue to support their emerging understanding of arrays.

❖ *Model as a tool for thinking*

The goal of this unit is only to introduce the array model. In third grade the unit *Muffles Truffles* develops a deeper understanding of the array model, including the open array model, and the unit *Tabletops, Floors, and Fields* extends the array model to a more formal understanding of area and perimeter. Eventually students become able to use the array model as a tool to think with—to prove and explore their ideas about multiplicative reasoning. Look for moments of puzzlement as students make arrays. Allowing students to decompose rectangles into sections and rearrange these sections into other arrays will help them develop a better understanding of the model. Don't hesitate to let students discuss their ideas and check and recheck their strategies. Celebrate their accomplishments! They are young mathematicians at work.

Graphics of the two landscapes of learning for this unit are provided on pages 14 and 15. The purpose of the graphics is to allow you to see the longer journey of students' geometric development and to place your work with *Little Cities* within the scope of this long-term development. You may also find the graphics helpful to record the progress of individual students for yourself. Each landmark can be shaded in as you find evidence in a student's work and in what the student says—evidence that a landmark strategy, big idea, or way of modeling has been constructed. If you prefer we also have a digital app with the glossary built-in (see www.NewPerspectivesOnAssessment.com for further information on this tool). In a sense, you will be recording the individual pathways your students take as they develop as young mathematicians.

References and Resources

Davies, Clare and David H. Uttal, 2007. Map use and the development of spatial cognition. In Jodie M. Plumert and John P. Spencer (eds.) *The Emerging Spatial Mind.* NY: Oxford University Press. pp. 219-247.

Dehaene, Stanislaus, Veronique Izard, Pierre Pica, and Elizabeth Spelke, 2006. Core knowledge of geometry in an Amazonian indigene group. *Science*. 311: 381-384.

Goodnow, Jacqueline, 1977. *Children Drawing*. Boston, MA: Harvard University Press.

Gravemeijer, Koeno P. E. 1999. How emergent models may foster the constitution of formal mathematics. *Mathematical Thinking and Learning 1* (2): 155–77.

Outhred, Lynn and Michael Mitchelmore, 2004. *Students' Structuring of Rectangular Arrays.* Paper presented in the Proceedings of the 28th Conference of the International Group for the Psychology of Mathematics Education. Vol 3 pp 465-472.

Piaget, Jean and Barbel Inhelder. 1967. *The Child's Conception of Space*. New York: Norton.

Spelke, Elizabeth, Sang Ah Lee, and Veronique Izard. 2010. Beyond core knowledge: natural geometry. *Cognitive Science*. May 1: 34 (5): 863-884.

van Hiele, Pierre. 1985 [1959]. *The Child's Thought and Geometry*, Brooklyn, NY: City University of New York, pp. 243–252.

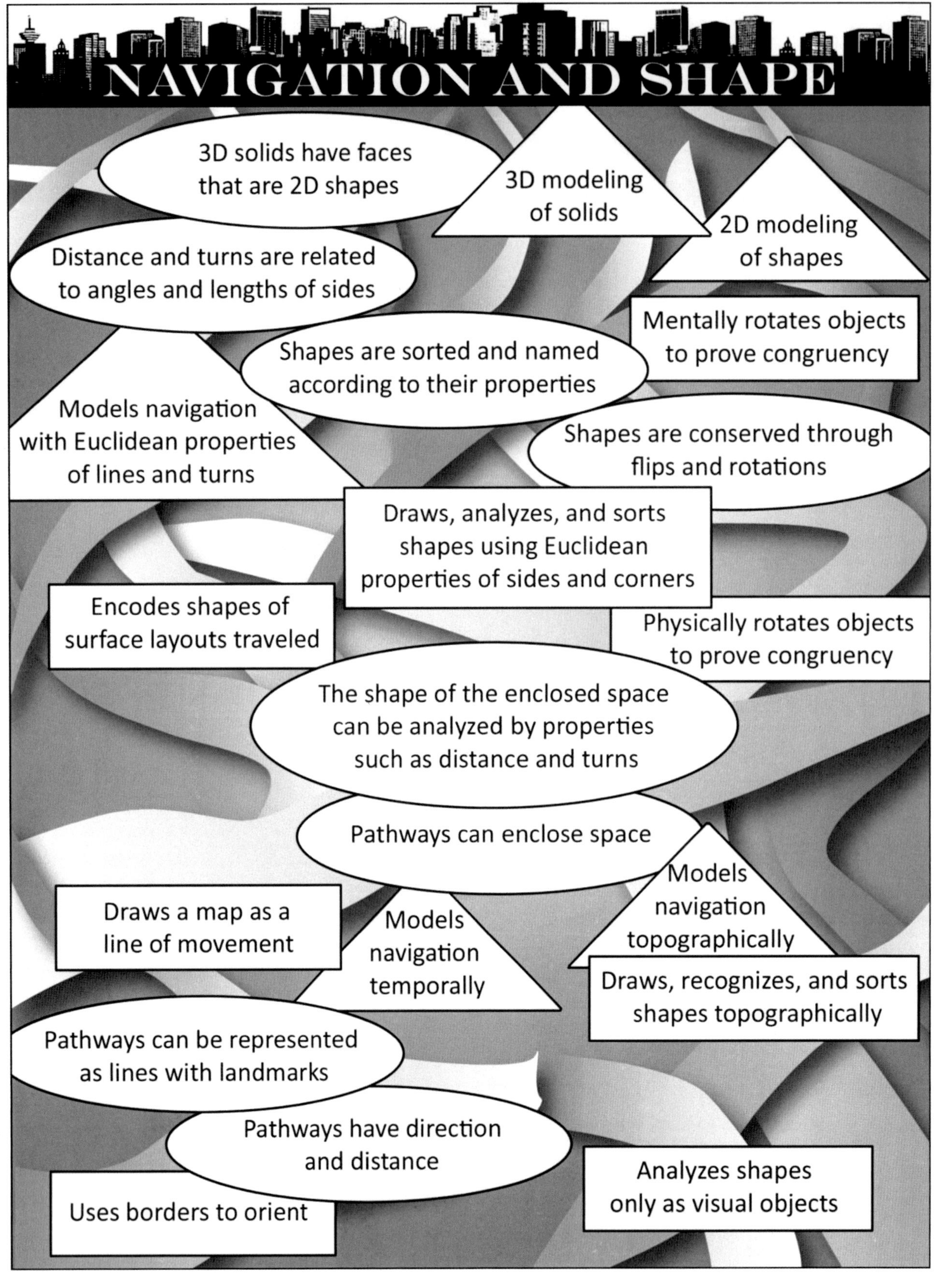

NAVIGATION AND SHAPE
3D solids have faces that are 2D shapes
3D modeling of solids
2D modeling of shapes
Distance and turns are related to angles and lengths of sides
Mentally rotates objects to prove congruency
Shapes are sorted and named according to their properties
Models navigation with Euclidean properties of lines and turns
Shapes are conserved through flips and rotations
Draws, analyzes, and sorts shapes using Euclidean properties of sides and corners
Encodes shapes of surface layouts traveled
Physically rotates objects to prove congruency
The shape of the enclosed space can be analyzed by properties such as distance and turns
Pathways can enclose space
Models navigation topographically
Draws a map as a line of movement
Models navigation temporally
Draws, recognizes, and sorts shapes topographically
Pathways can be represented as lines with landmarks
Pathways have direction and distance
Analyzes shapes only as visual objects
Uses borders to orient

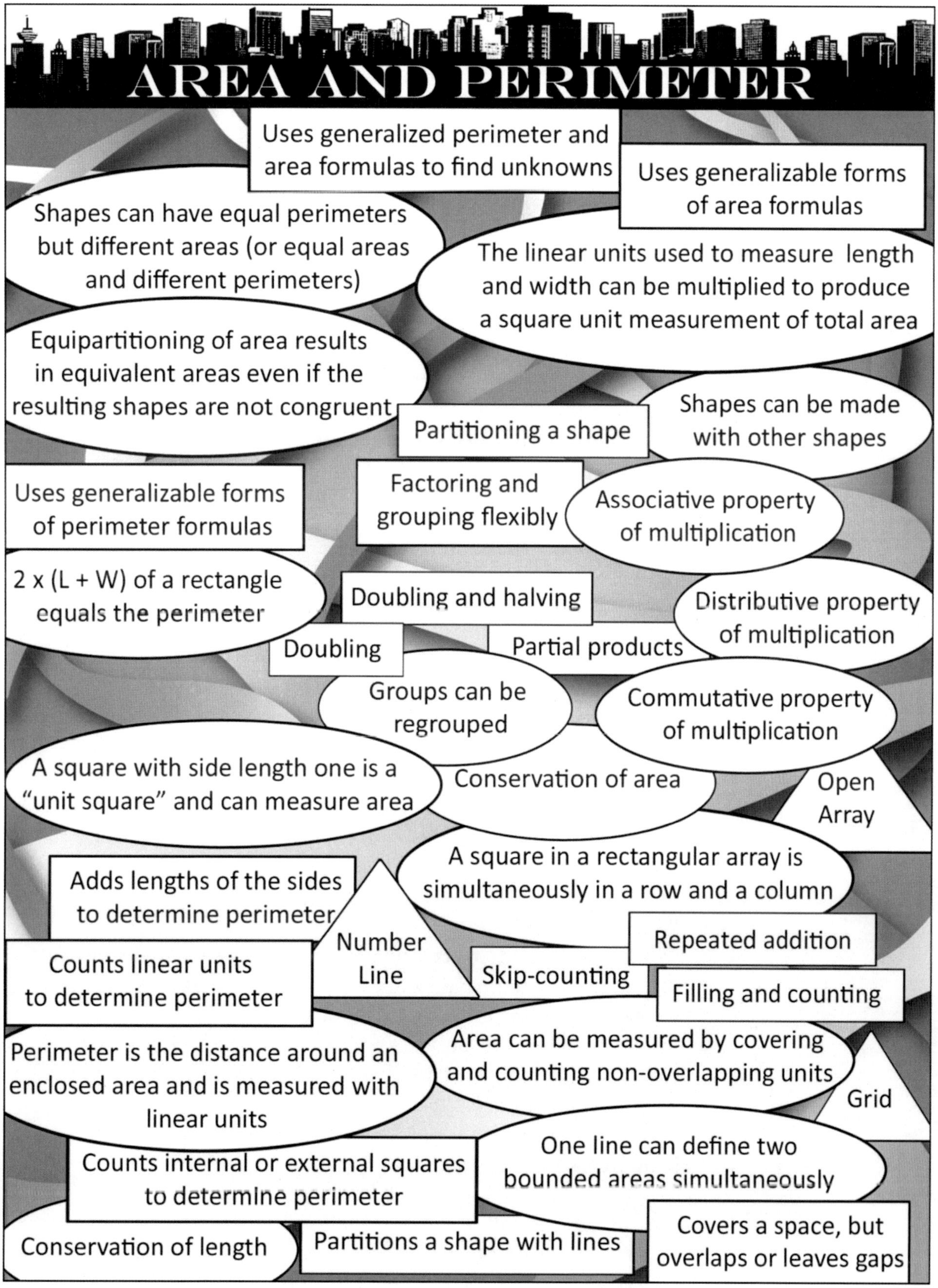

AREA AND PERIMETER

Uses generalized perimeter and area formulas to find unknowns

Uses generalizable forms of area formulas

Shapes can have equal perimeters but different areas (or equal areas and different perimeters)

The linear units used to measure length and width can be multiplied to produce a square unit measurement of total area

Equipartitioning of area results in equivalent areas even if the resulting shapes are not congruent

Partitioning a shape

Shapes can be made with other shapes

Uses generalizable forms of perimeter formulas

Factoring and grouping flexibly

Associative property of multiplication

2 x (L + W) of a rectangle equals the perimeter

Doubling and halving

Distributive property of multiplication

Doubling

Partial products

Groups can be regrouped

Commutative property of multiplication

A square with side length one is a "unit square" and can measure area

Conservation of area

Open Array

A square in a rectangular array is simultaneously in a row and a column

Adds lengths of the sides to determine perimeter

Number Line

Repeated addition

Counts linear units to determine perimeter

Skip-counting

Filling and counting

Perimeter is the distance around an enclosed area and is measured with linear units

Area can be measured by covering and counting non-overlapping units

Grid

Counts internal or external squares to determine perimeter

One line can define two bounded areas simultaneously

Conservation of length

Partitions a shape with lines

Covers a space, but overlaps or leaves gaps

DAY ONE

MAPPING OUT A CITY PLAN

Materials Needed

City Streets (Appendix A, one copy per child with extras for revisions)

Pattern Blocks (a set of 4 orange squares, 1 yellow hexagon, 2 green triangles, 3 blue rhombi, and 2 red trapezoids, one set per pair of students)

Quick Images (Appendix B)

Math Journals

Pencils

The day begins with a minilesson on analyzing and sorting polygons by their properties. Then a context of making a model of a small city is introduced and using pattern blocks, students outline building footprints and decide where to place them along city streets. The number of sides and the number of turns are recorded for each and students are asked to imagine what the shape of the building will be as it gains in height. Through drawing and recording, students explore and are encouraged to imagine 2-D shapes being transformed into 3-D prisms.

Day One Outline

Minilesson: Quick Images

❖ Show one quick image from Appendix B at a time and invite students to share the name of the polygon they saw.

❖ Invite discussion on the properties and sort each image by the number of sides and corners as you go.

❖ At the end of the minilesson you should have only 3 groups. Label them triangles, quadrilaterals, and hexagons and provide discussion on how squares, trapezoids, and rhombi are all four-sided polygons, and thus quadrilaterals.

Developing the Context

❖ Invite students to talk about small models of towns or cities they may have seen and explain that over the next week the class will be building one using a variety of shapes.

❖ Ask students to design small sections of a city using pattern blocks and to make outlines of the foundations of buildings they want on their streets.

Supporting the Investigation

❖ Note students' strategies as they draw their maps and elicit and discuss their different explanations for how the shapes were made, focusing on the properties of the shapes.

❖ Have students record their data in their journals.

Minilesson: Quick Images

Gather the children around you in a meeting area. Explain that you will be doing "quick images." Draw three circles labeled by number of sides and corners. The first circle should say 3 sides and 3 corners; the second, 4 sides and 4 corners; and the third, 6 sides and 6 corners. Show one card at a time from Appendix B, moving it from your right to your left, then behind your back. With each card ask, *"What did you see and how many sides and corners does it have?"* After discussion on the shape seen, ask students which circle the shape goes in. Allow students to name the shape if they know it, but don't push the term "quadrilateral" at this point unless a student offers it. Since quadrilaterals have 4 sides and 4 angles, rectangles (including squares), rhombi, and trapezoids will all end up in the second circle no matter what the shape is named. You will be introducing the term, quadrilateral, at the end of the minilesson once all the shapes are sorted.

Show image #1 from Appendix B for a few seconds and then remove it. Ask the children to notice the number of sides and corners it has, then ask them to turn and tell their neighbor what they saw. Invite a few children to share their answers focusing the discussion on the number of sides and corners and then move the shape to the circle it belongs in, sorting the shapes by their properties. After you present image #2 ask for answers, and while students are still looking at it, rotate the shape so that the sides are oriented vertically and horizontally. With image #8, in front of the children cut along a diagonal effectively dividing the hexagon into two trapezoids. Ask which circle these go in. Trapezoids have 4 sides.

Behind the Crafting of the Minilesson

The string starts with an easily recognized shape in a common orientation. Image 2 is the same triangle, rotated 180 degrees. Students may call this a "cone" or an "upside-down triangle." A goal is to get them to see that it is the three corners that make it a triangle, not the orientation, so for now just focus conversation on how many sides and corners the shape has. Image #4 is a rhombus (a quadrilateral with equal length sides). Image #5 is also a rhombus, but it is also a square because the angles are right angles. It is also a quadrilateral because it is a closed shape with 4 sides. Image #8 when it is cut will result in two trapezoids, which each have 4 sides and 4 corners. Once the shapes are all sorted, invite discussion on why the shapes can look different but still be in the same circle. Support students to understand that shapes are sorted by their properties and label the three circles: triangles, quadrilaterals, and hexagons.

The string of shapes:

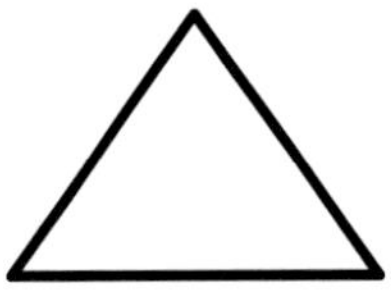

Image #1:

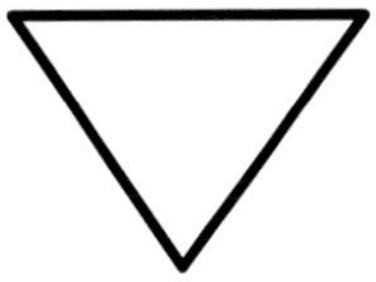

Image #2:

Image #3

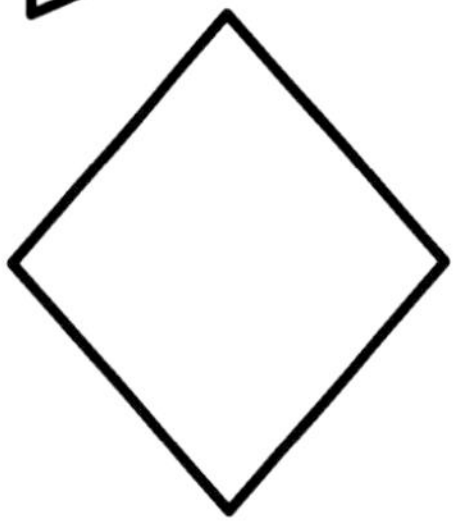

Image #4:

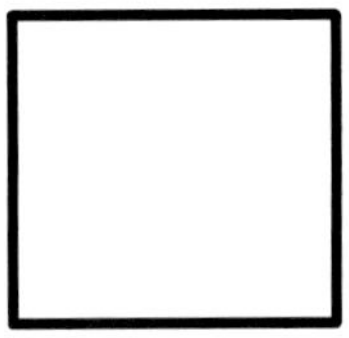

Image #5:

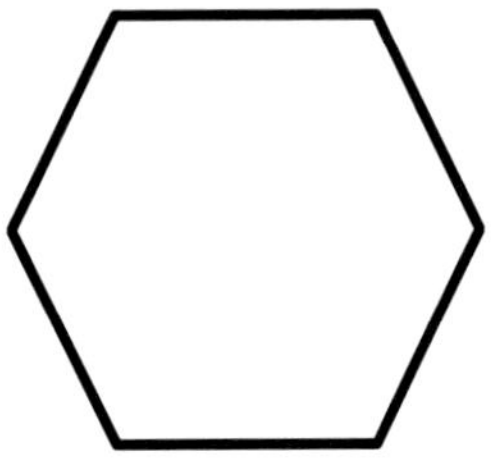

Image #6:

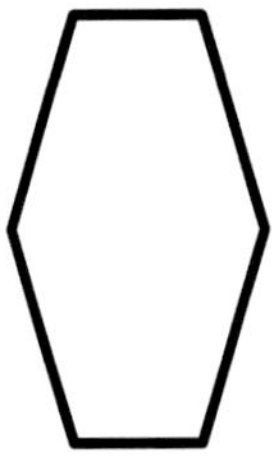

Image #7:

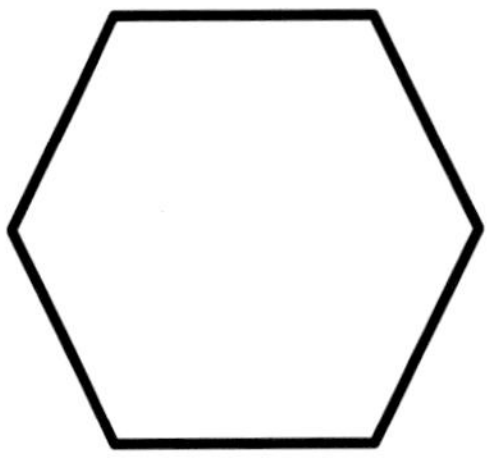

Image #8:

Developing the Context

Begin developing the context by inviting students to discuss what they know about miniature towns and/or cities. Have they ever seen one, or built one? What is involved in working on such a small scale? Is it difficult, but fun?

Explain that over the next week the class will be involved in the building of a little city and math partners will start today by working together to design and map out a small section.

> **Teacher Note:**
>
> **If you google "miniature towns" you will likely find several short videos that you can use to develop the context, as there are several miniature towns that have been built around the world. Madurodam in the Netherlands is one of the most famous. Many children will likely also have experiences with building**

Display Appendix A as an example and demonstrate on a copy of it how students should start today by making a sectional map of the city that they wish to design. Using the pattern block possibilities shown below, each student should choose a few designs and outline footprints of 3 or 4 possible buildings. [Note how orange pattern blocks can be placed together to make a 2 x 2 square base for a building (or a 1 x 2 or 1 x 3 non-square rectangular base). The orange blocks can also be used separately for some smaller buildings.] When you are done, you might have something like the plan shown on Appendix A, in the figure below (the placement of your shapes can be different). **[Outlines must be quadrilaterals, triangles, or hexagons only.]**

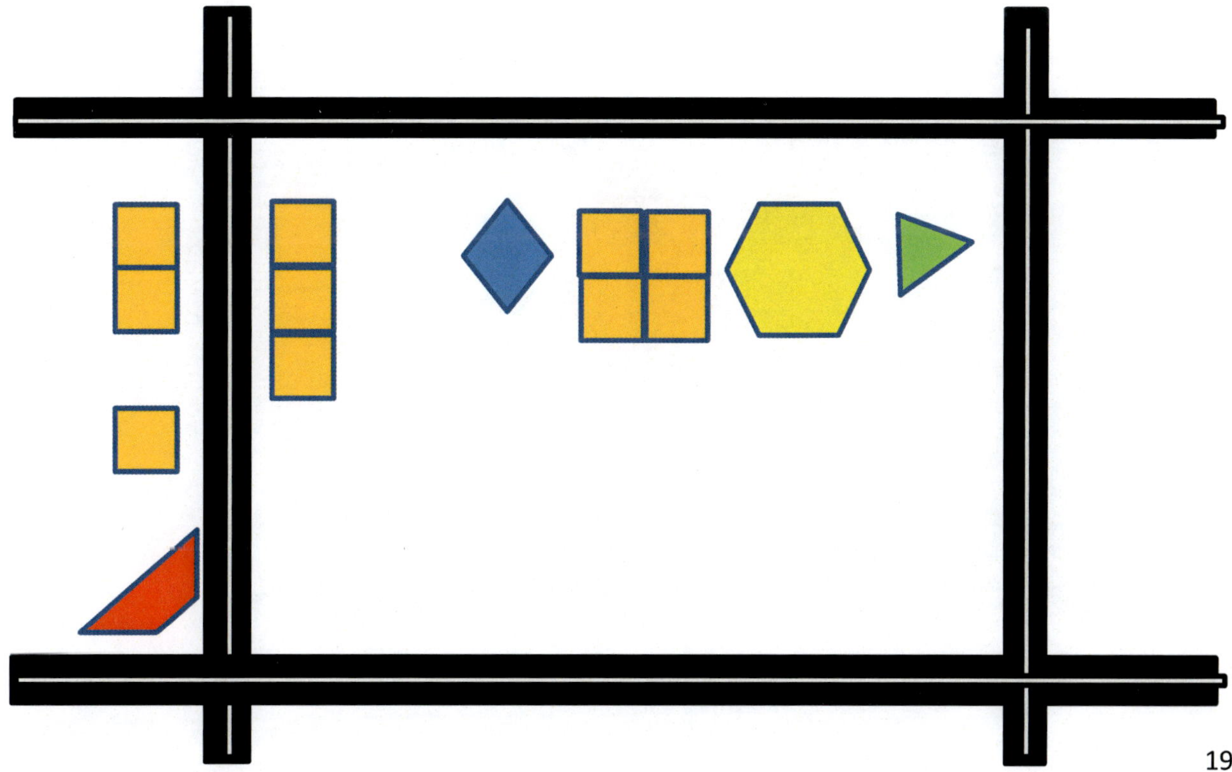

Once students understand the goal of the day's task, formulate pairs, provide each pair with a set of pattern blocks, pencils, and each student with a copy of Appendix A, and send them off to design a map of a city block showing the footprints (outlines of the foundation) of the buildings that will eventually go there.

Supporting the Investigation

As students work, move around the room and confer as needed to support and challenge their investigation. As students use the pattern blocks to outline the footprints (or foundations) of the buildings, encourage them to imagine what the shape of the building will be when floors are added—when the model of the full 3-D building is built. You can introduce new vocabulary at this point explaining that the buildings will all be what mathematicians call *prisms.* The prisms have multi-stacked levels of the footprint shape and the top of each building will also have a flat deck the same shape as the footprint.

Some students may begin by trying to trace around the pattern block in one move without lifting their pencil. They may still be thinking of the shape primarily as topological space—an outline of rounded closed space—rather than a shape comprised of line segments and angles. See Figure 1. The trapezoid in the upper middle is particularly telling. As you confer with students like these, point out the four sides and suggest they might try drawing each, one-at-a-time. Note also in Figure 1 how all borders of the two squares are drawn. One line is not yet understood as a border of two regions simultaneously.

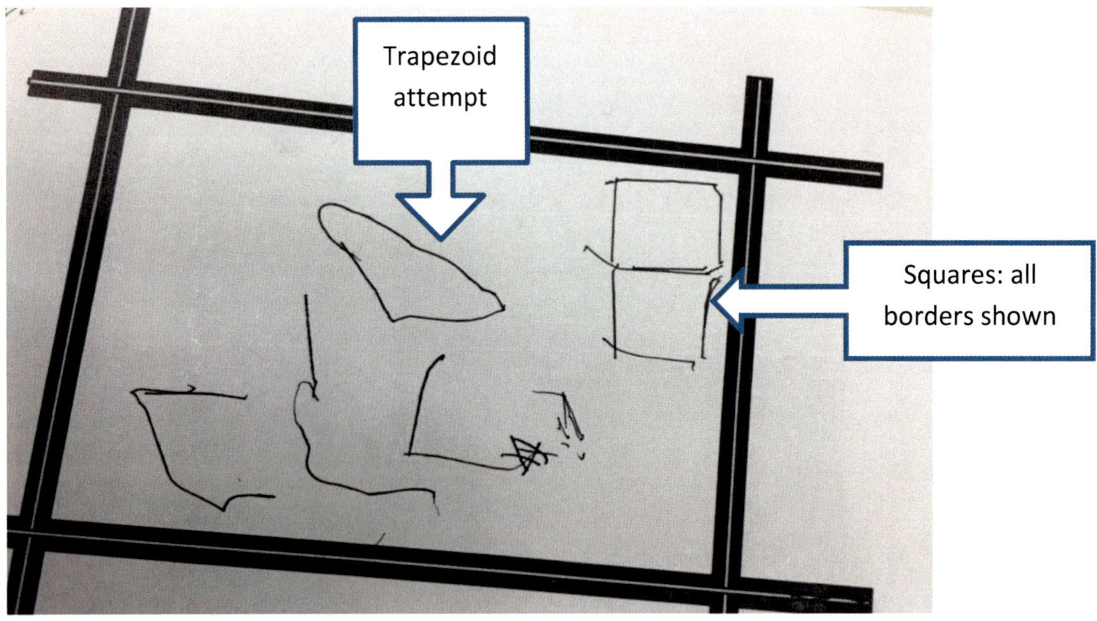

Figure 1

Other students may use a block to fill space repeatedly, thereby making a footprint like the one shown in Figure 2. As you confer, remind them that the building footprints must be triangles, quadrilaterals, or hexagons and support them to count the number of sides. See the dialogue box that follows.

Figure 2

<table>
<tr><th colspan="2">Inside One Classroom: Conferring with Students at Work</th></tr>
<tr><td>

Tammie (the teacher): Wow! This is a big building, isn't it! May I sit and confer with you?

Kristin: Sure. I'm making it with squares. A square is a quada....What's that called again?

Tammie: A quadrilateral. A square does have 4 sides and 4 corners. I see that! And I see that you are putting them together to make a different shape. How many sides does your new big shape have?

Kristin: 1, 2, 3, 4, 5, 6.... (counting the squares).

</td><td>

Author's notes

Tammie sees what Kristin is doing. By placing the

</td></tr>
</table>

Tammie: Not how many squares... How many sides? When we fold the paper around this shape tomorrow to make our buildings, how many sides will this building have? **Kristin:** (looking puzzled and starts to count the squares again.) **Tammie:** Some of those squares are going to be inside the basement, I think. Let's trace an outline of the building so we can see the shape better. Then we can count the sides. (*Tammie traces the outline*) and helps Kristin count the sides, starting with the square on the bottom right. 1, 2, 3, 4, (and then she moves her finger across, down, and to the left) 5, 6, 7... I think this building is going to have a lot of sides. It's not going to be a quadrilateral. They only have 4 sides, right? **Kristin:** Oh yeah. Can I start over? **Tammie:** Of course. It is very helpful to make drafts. That's how we get good ideas! Here is another sheet.	*squares together, she is confusing the sides of the square with the sides of the new building she is making.* *Tammie supports Kristin to see the outline of the new shape and counts the sides with her. This move causes disequilibrium about what a side is and fosters some thinking on the part/whole relations. A big idea is at play here: shapes can be made with other shapes.* *Tammie knows drafts and revisions should be encouraged. This is an important part of doing mathematics!*

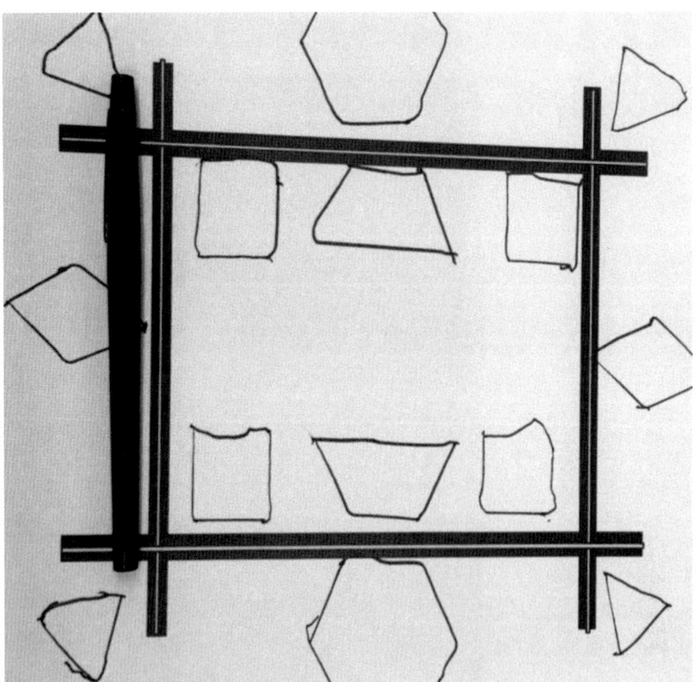

Figure 3

Figure 3 on the left shows the more Euclidean approach that you want to encourage. Note how the properties, line segments, and angles are being used. This student has even decided to use symmetry in his city design!

If not all the children use an approach like this on day one, don't be concerned. Tomorrow, when they attempt to fold the nets to make their buildings, they will discover the problems themselves when the nets don't fit. Just remember to allow fresh starts for more drafts and revisions, as doing so supports learning!

As students finish working on their designs, ask them to make journal entries about the shapes of the footprints they made and to draw what they think the sides (the faces) of their buildings will look like so they can imagine where windows will go. Explain that tomorrow they will be making sides and adding windows to their buildings, so planning and thinking about that work ahead will be helpful.

> **Math Note:**
>
> Because of the shape of the pattern blocks being traced, the buildings will be rectangular prisms, cubes, triangular prisms, trapezoidal prisms, rhomboid prisms, and hexagonal prisms. But at this point don't give this away. Students may have difficulty imagining the shapes at this point. As they work this week, they will have many opportunities to see the polygon footprints transformed into prisms with their own eyes. Allow students to be surprised.

Take the journals home tonight and read through them. Write back to your students in the journals. The comments do not need to be long. A few sentences will do. Conversing individually with students in their journals is a great way to support students to write about their mathematics. You are providing them with an audience. Now they are not just writing because you told them to; they are writing to you and will look forward to what you say in response. Writers need audiences! A few journal entries are provided in Figures 4-6 to help you anticipate what your students might do.

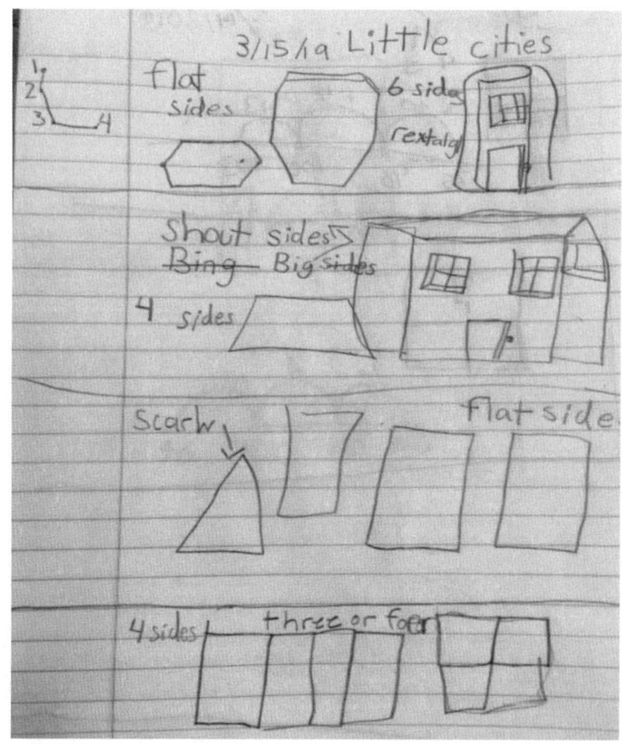

Figure 4

Figure 5

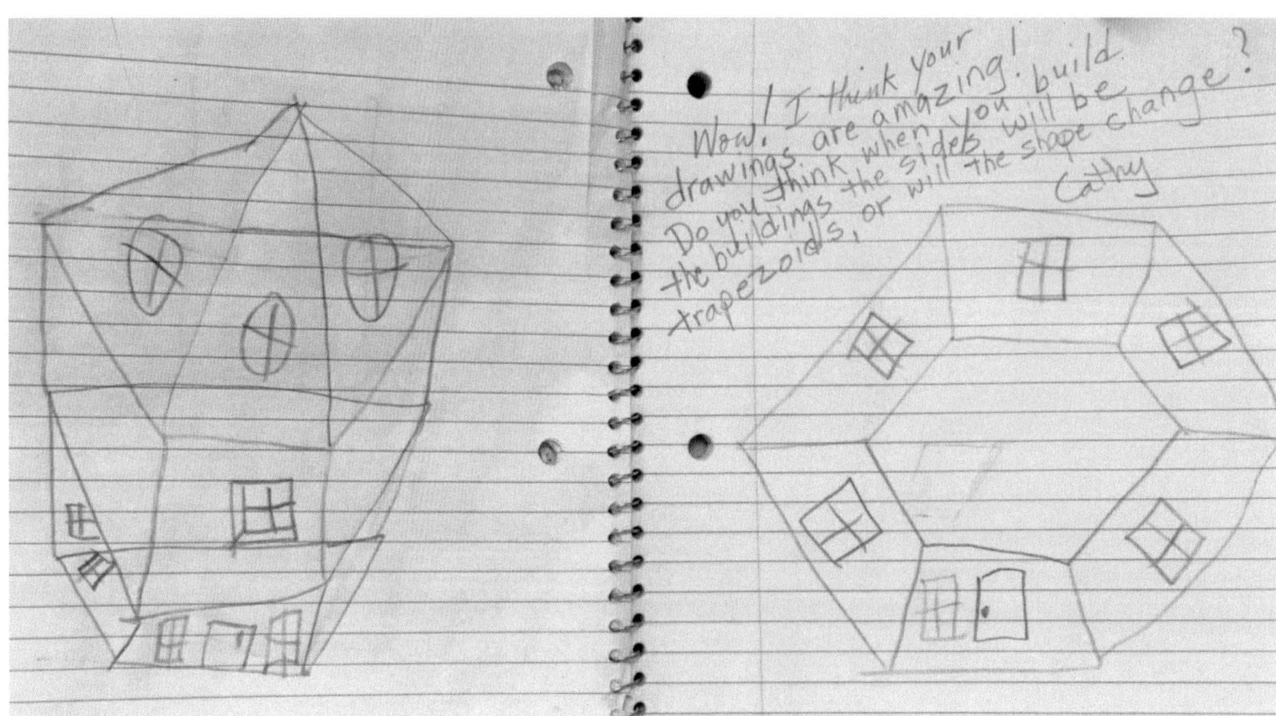

Figure 6

Reflections on the Day

Students explored several big ideas today about properties of two-dimensional shapes as they discussed the footprints of their buildings and plotted out their city designs. The context investigated today was a powerful one for beginning the journey of constructing 3-D prisms using familiar 2-D shapes. Tomorrow, students will continue with this work. Using nets and folding they will begin the work of making their 3-D models. Save the work from each day, take some pictures, and make note of the conversations you hear so that you will have lots of nice examples to use on a learning scroll at the end of the unit.

DAY TWO

FROM 2-D FOOTPRINTS TO 3-D MODELS

The day begins again with a similar minilesson to the one yesterday on analyzing and sorting polygons by their properties. Then students work with nets, folding and taping them around the pattern blocks to make 3-D models of small buildings for their cities.

Materials Needed

Quick Image Shapes (Appendix C)

Nets for the Buildings (Appendix D, extra copies available as needed)

Pattern Blocks (a set of 4 orange squares, 1 yellow hexagon, 2 green triangles, 3 blue rhombi, and 2 red trapezoids (one set per pair of students)

Work from Day One (with extra copies of Appendix A if needed)

Math Journals

Pencils

Tape

Scissors

Day Two Outline

Minilesson: Quick Images

❖ Show one image from Appendix C at a time as a quick image and invite students to share what they saw.

❖ Invite discussion on the properties and sort each image by the number of sides and corners as you go.

❖ At the end of the minilesson you should have only 3 groups. Label them triangles, quadrilaterals, and hexagons and provide discussion on how the shapes can look very different but still go in the same category when sorted.

Developing the Context

❖ Explain that today students will be building up from the footprints and will be making 3-D shapes to represent buildings.

❖ Provide nets (Appendix D) and show children how they can be folded and taped to fit around the pattern blocks.

❖ Invite students to make windows on the sides of their buildings before taping them in place.

Supporting the Investigation

❖ Note students' strategies as they fold the net and discuss with them how the number of sides of the polygon footprints and the number of faces needed are related.

❖ Where appropriate focus discussion on halves, thirds, fourths, and sixths.

Minilesson: Quick Images

As you did yesterday at the start of math workshop, gather the children around you in a meeting area and explain that you will again be doing "quick images." Draw three circles labeled by number of sides and corners. As yesterday, the first circle should say 3 sides and 3 corners; the second, 4 sides and 4 corners; and the third, 6 sides and 6 corners. Show one card at a time from Appendix C, moving it from your right to your left, then behind your back. With each card ask, "*What did you see and how many sides and corners does it have?*" After discussion on the shape seen and the properties, ask students which circle the shape goes in.

Show image #1 from Appendix C for a few seconds and then remove it. Ask the children to consider the name of the polygon, but more importantly to notice the number of sides and corners it has, then ask them to turn and tell their neighbor which shape they saw and how they knew it was that shape. Invite a few children to share their answers focusing the discussion on the number of sides and corners and then move the shape to the circle it belongs in, sorting the shapes by their properties.

The string of shapes:

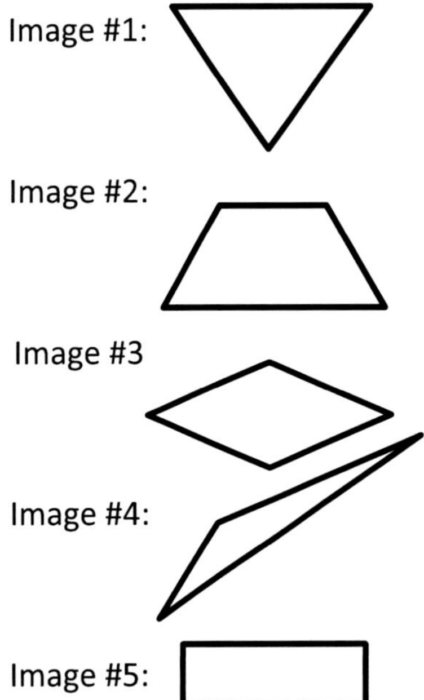

Behind the Crafting of the Minilesson

The shapes shown today are a little more challenging than those used yesterday. The string starts with a triangle in an orientation that was discussed yesterday, one that has been rotated 180 degrees from the more commonly shown image. Images #6 and #7 are both hexagons, but several students may be challenged to see this. Focus the discussion on the number of straight lines and the number of corners. Once the shapes are all sorted, invite discussion on why the shapes can look different but still be in the same category. Support students to understand that shapes are sorted by their properties and once again label the three groups: triangles, quadrilaterals, and hexagons. Students may argue that the scalene triangle is not a triangle. Image #7 may also prove challenging for students to accept that it is a hexagon, because it has one angle greater than 180 degrees making it a concave hexagon. Explain that shapes are named by the number of sides and angles (corners) they have, not by what they look like.

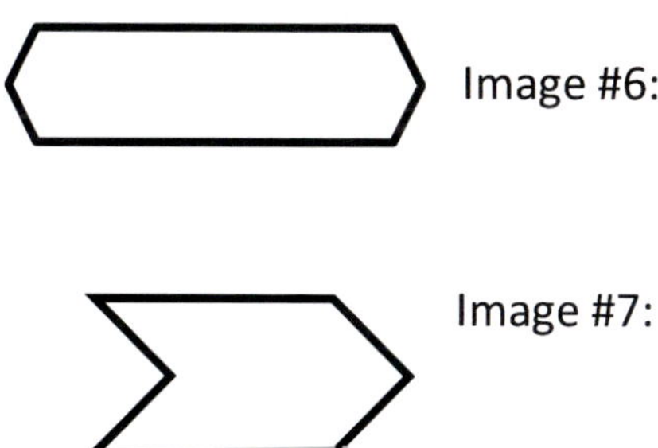

Developing the Context

Display the first net from Appendix D (the triangular prism net) and invite students to consider which building footprint they think it might go with when it is folded. If they are challenged by this, ask them to consider how the net might be folded to go around three equal sides. Remind students that the triangle has 3 sides and demonstrate how the net can be folded into thirds on the dotted lines and by using the edge of the green pattern block to measure the 3 equal pieces. Introduce the term *thirds* and write the fraction 1/3, explaining that the notation means 1 divided into 3 *equal* pieces. Fold the net along each dotted line and tape it closed, then tape the triangular lid down and fit the prism over the pattern block. Tape the bottom to hold the pattern block in place. Explain that the buildings will all have flat roofs for roof decks and help students see that in this case the roof deck is also a triangle. The building should look like the figure shown in Figure 7 when you are done.

Explain that you are going to give them copies of nets that they can use to make a variety of buildings, which they can then put on the 2-D footprints that they made yesterday. Suggest that they draw in windows and doors first though, before they fold and tape.

Figure 7: a triangular prism

Supporting the Investigation

As students work, move around the room and confer as needed to support and challenge their investigation. As students draw and color windows and doors, encourage them to consider which side of the shape will be the top. Invite discussion on the shape of each face and encourage students to note how each lateral face of the building (each side) is a rectangle no matter what the polygon of the footprint is. And, the top deck of each building is the same as the footprint.

Inside One Classroom: Conferring with Students at Work	
***Julio and Crystal** have cut out the net for the trapezoidal prism and are discussing where the windows and door should go.*	
Julio: The building must fit over the pattern block when we are done folding so the door can't be there. That is the top, where the roof deck goes. See? This trapezoid folds over, and we tape it here after we make our windows. If you put a door there, it will be hanging upside down from the roof!	*Author's notes*
Crystal: Oh yeah. Ok. I'll turn it around.	
Tammie (the teacher): Good noticing, you two! There is a lot to think about as we make our 3-D models, isn't there? I noticed when you made the building for the square and the rhombus footprints that you were discussing that the big rectangle on the net was being folded both times into fourths. Will that happen with the trapezoid, too? It has 4 sides, too, right?	*Tammie starts the conferral by celebrating what Julio and Crystal have noticed. Then she challenges with a question that causes them to consider lengths of the sides of the quadrilaterals, not just the number of sides.*
Crystal: I think it will. It is a quadrilateral, too.	
Tammie: What do you think, Julio?	
Julio: I'm not sure. There are four parts, but they look different.	*This is a moment to heighten reflection on fractions. Four parts does not necessarily mean fourths. To be fourths, the parts must be equal.*
Tammie: Why would that be? Let's look at the trapezoid. Are the sides different lengths?	
Julio: Oh yeah. That's why (smiling)! One side is longer! There are four sides, but they aren't the same lengths.	

Tammie: Ah! And to be fourths, the parts must be *equal*, so these aren't fourths! What shapes will the faces of the sides of the building be? **Crystal:** Rectangles, but different ones, I think. See, it's like this bigger rectangle (*pointing to the net*) has been cut into 4 smaller rectangles and they aren't the same sizes. This one is wider, but the others are the same. **Tammie:** Interesting! These three are congruent! Look, they match; that's what congruent means. And you are right! The other face is quite different. It is much wider. It's interesting to see how the lengths of the sides of the footprint affect the faces of the building, isn't it? This might be a nice focus for your poster!	*Crystal notes that three of the lateral faces are alike and Tammie introduces the word "congruent" naturally. At the same time, she brings into focus how the properties of the trapezoid are affecting the shape of the faces of the prism.*

As math workshop draws to a close for the day, invite students to reflect in their journals on some of the things they noted today about how the shape of the footprint affects the number of faces and the shape of the faces of the building. Tomorrow will start with peer review groups where students will share their journal entries from today.

Reflections on the Day

In the minilesson today, students analyzed 2-D shapes by their properties and sorted them. Then they explored how the properties of the two-dimensional shapes of the footprints affected the 3-D prisms. It would be a great idea to take the math journals home this evening again to see and comment on what your students have written in them. This is a great way to gain insights into the big ideas that students are generating, and it will help you prepare for an interesting discussion in the congress tomorrow. Students also love getting even short notes back from you and they look forward to reading what you write. Dialogue journals are a powerful way to encourage students to write more. After all, they love having you as their audience!

DAY THREE

WHAT SHAPES ARE THE FACES?

Materials Needed

Math Journals

Student Work from days one and two

Chart or drawing paper for posters

Markers

Extra copies of nets as needed (Appendix D)

Sticky Notes for use in the Gallery Walk

Scissors

Tape

Students review their journal entries and then meet in small groups for peer review. They discuss the shapes of the faces of the buildings and discuss why the faces are all rectangles, as well as other regularities they may have noticed. They resume work and then make posters for a gallery walk and congress. The finished posters are placed around the room for review and a subsequent congress is held to discuss a few of the big ideas that have emerged as they worked.

Day Three Outline

Preparing for the Gallery Walk

❖ Students review their journal entries from the day before and then meet in peer review groups to discuss their findings on the shapes of the faces of their buildings.

❖ Students resume work and then create posters about the shapes of the faces of the buildings and other interesting things they have noted.

Facilitating the Gallery Walk

❖ Conduct a gallery walk to allow students time to reflect and comment on each other's posters.

Facilitating Math Congress

❖ Choose a few posters that will generate a discussion on how the shapes of the faces are affected by the base (footprint) of the building. All are rectangles but they differ in size, depending on the lengths and number of sides of the polygonal base. The larger rectangle in the net is folded into sections, sometimes equal sections, sometimes not. Use this observation for a discussion on fractions.

Preparing for the Gallery Walk

Begin by having students review the notes they made in their journals yesterday and then form peer review groups by having 2 pairs of students come together to discuss what they have noticed about the faces of the buildings they have made thus far. As you walk around and listen into conversations, look for the following:

- note which students have noticed that all faces are rectangles and that they differ in size, depending on what polygon has been used as a base. Support them to explain why and suggest that this is an important idea to write a poster on.
- Look for students who can talk about how the sizes of the sides of the prisms differ at times: some faces are congruent, and some are not. Support discussion on how the rectangle in the net is folded equally when the sides of the polygon are equal, discussing the whole as 3/3, or 4/4, depending on the polygonal base.
- If some students have built a trapezoidal and/or non-square rectangular prism, support discussion on how there are 4 parts, but the parts are not equal and therefore they aren't fourths. Only the square and the rhombus are made from fourths.

After sufficient discussion in the small groups, have students return to work on the building of their little cities. This extra work time is important. First, students are likely engaged in the making of the cities and will want to make more buildings; but secondly, this time provides reflection on the discussions they have just had. As students return to work, move around and confer and help them notice some of the things that were discussed in their small peer review groups. Once each student has made several buildings and added them to their little city models, encourage students to work with a partner and begin making a poster of the important things they have noticed about how the 3-D models relate to the 2-D models. Several examples of posters are shown from our field-testing site for your review to help you anticipate what your students might do.

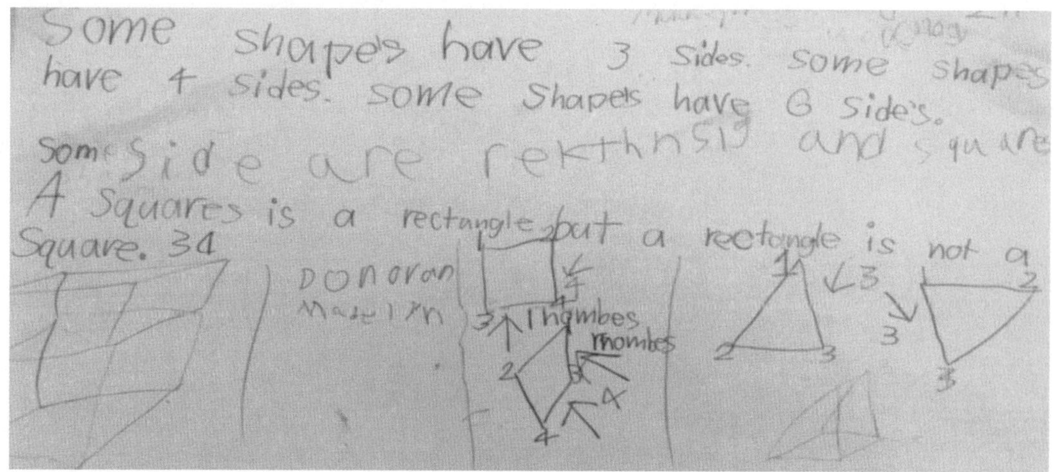

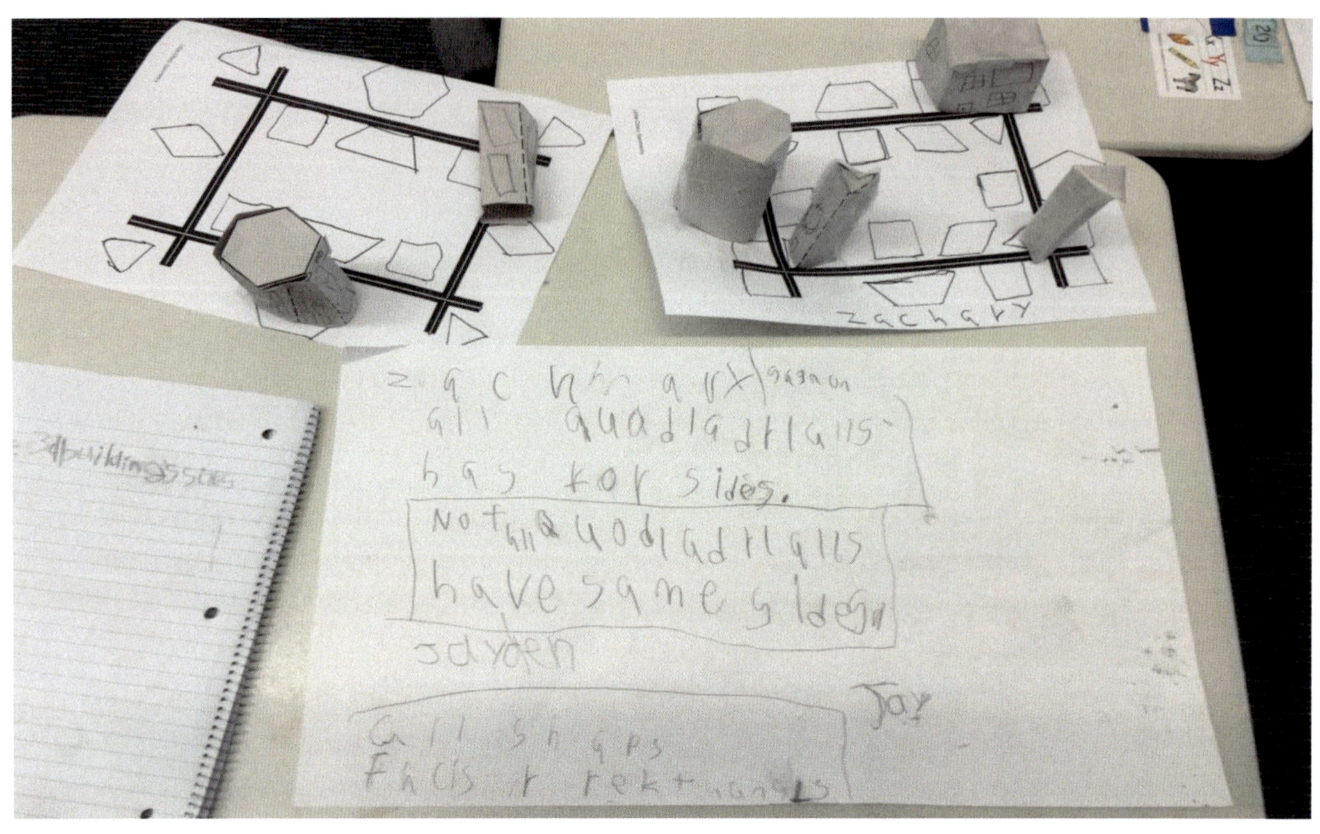
zachary
has for sides.
Jay

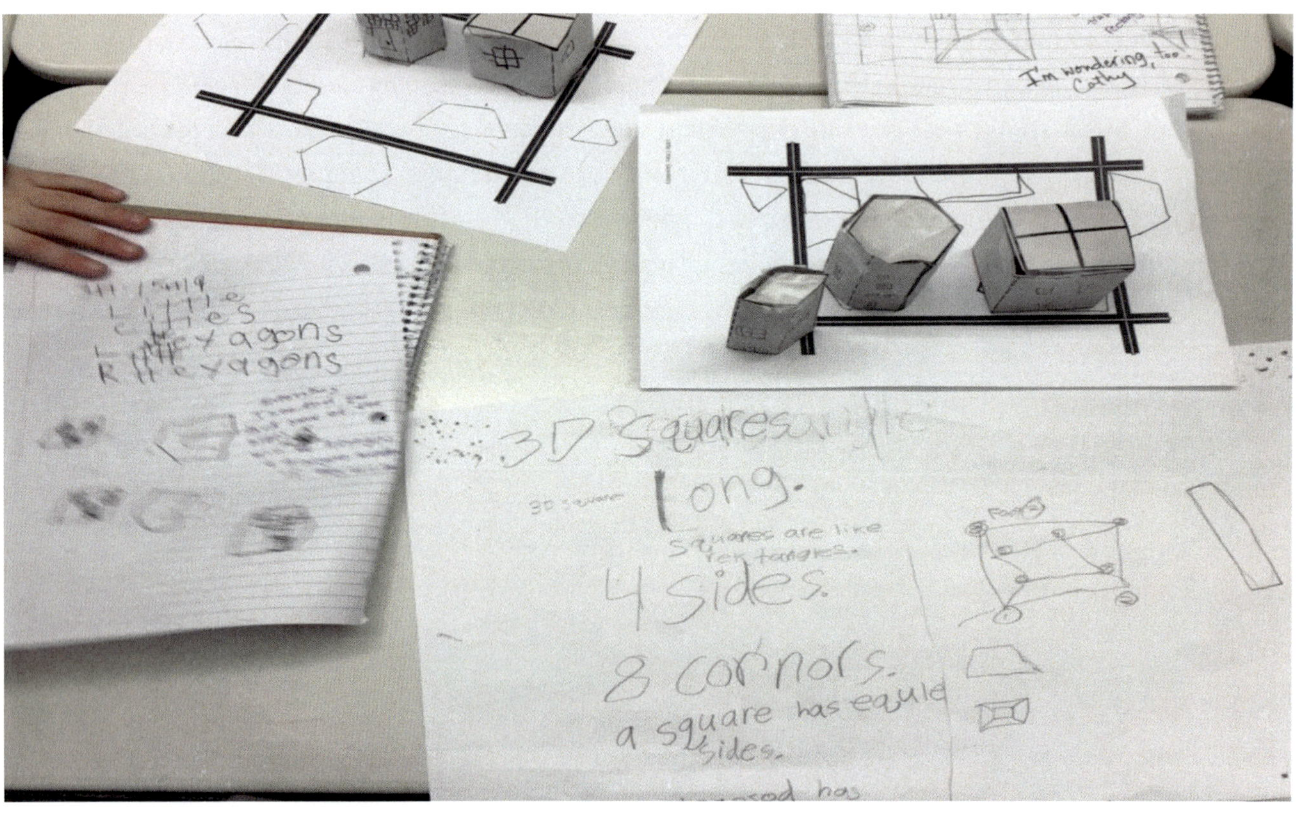
I'm wondering, too.
Cathy
3D Squares
long.
4 sides.
8 cornors.
a square has equule sides.

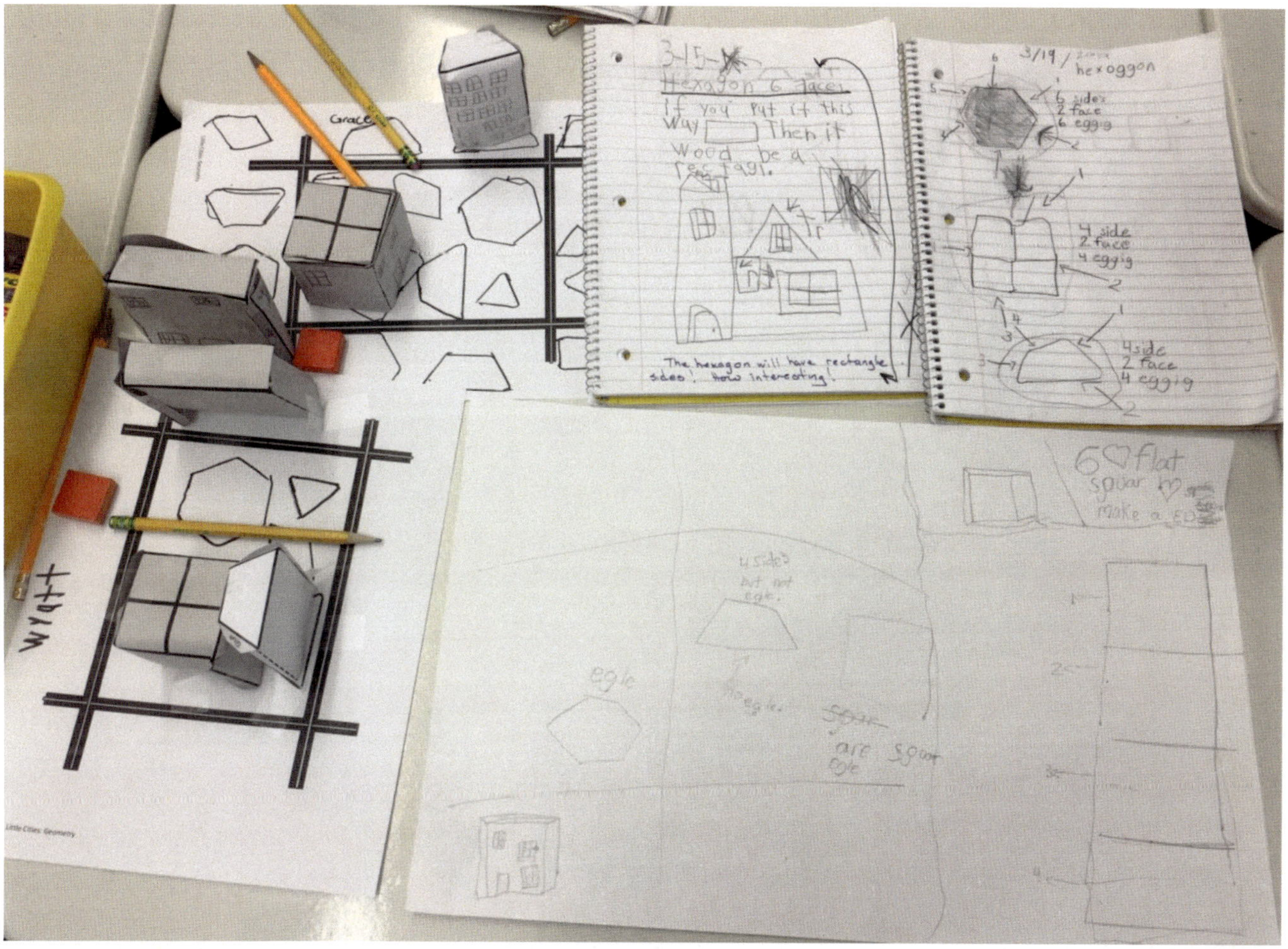

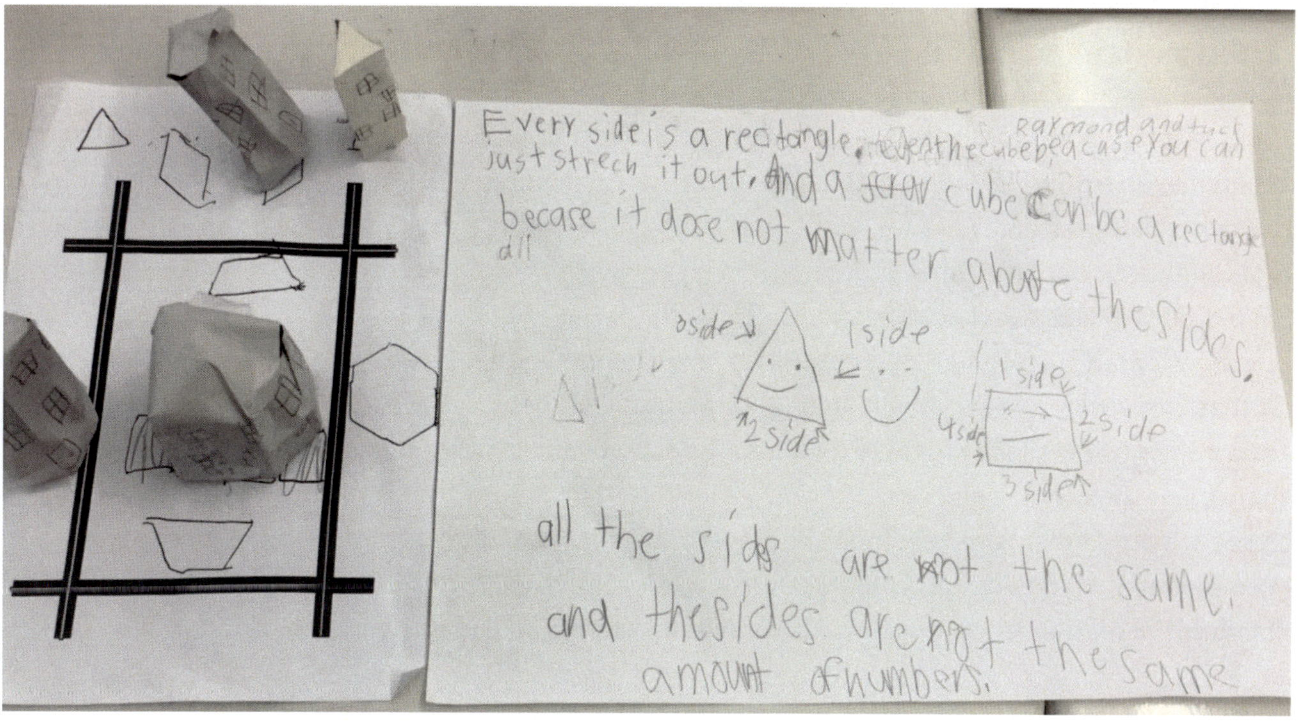
Every side is a rectangle
just strech it out, and a cube can be a rectangle
becase it dose not matter about the sides.
0side
1side
2side
1side
2side
3side
4side
all the sids are not the same.
and the sides are not the same
amount of numbers.

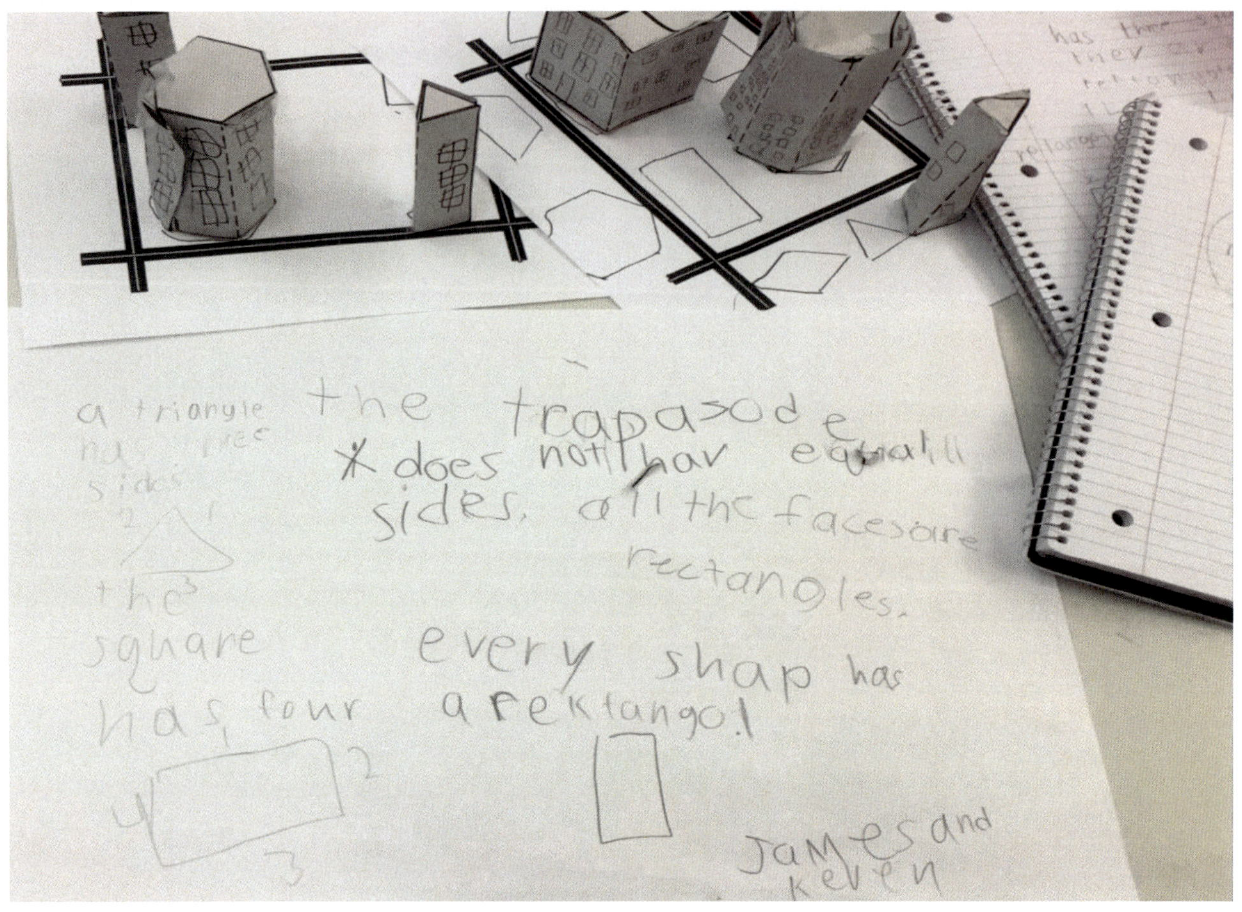

For the gallery walk, it is probably best to spread the posters and city models out on tables or on the floor. A level surface will provide more stability and protect the model buildings from falling over. Pass out sticky notes for use when reviewing and suggest that students walk around and read what others have written on their posters and leave review comments. Explain to your students that during a gallery walk they will walk around and look at the other posters and will have an important job: can they understand what another group is showing on their poster? As they walk around, they should be thinking, "Do I understand this?" "Is this what I noticed? Do I agree, disagree, or have questions about what this group wrote? Also, explain that during the gallery walk there is no talking so that everyone can read, think, and write helpful comments. Have students walk around and review the posters silently for 5-10 minutes. They should make comments on sticky notes and leave them on posters for the authors. After the gallery walk, invite the groups to go back to their posters to see what comments were left on their poster. By having this gallery walk, you are encouraging your students to reflect and comment on written and visual forms of mathematics, one of the standards of mathematical practice. It's something professional mathematicians do!

This is a good time for you to consider which posters you'll use in the following congress. You'll want to focus discussion on viable arguments for why all faces of the buildings are rectangles, and why they differ in size and depend on what polygon has been used as a base. A second important idea for discussion is that when the lengths of the sides of the polygon are equal, the big rectangle in the net is being folded into fractional pieces. For example, when the base of the building is an equilateral triangle, the rectangle is being folded into thirds and thus the whole rectangle being folded can be considered as 3/3. When the base is a square or a rhombus, the folding results in fourths and the whole is then 4/4. When the base is a regular hexagon, the rectangle is being folded into sixths and thus the whole is 6/6. Lastly, look for a poster that includes work with the trapezoid and a variety of non-square rectangles so that you can promote discussion on how the folding results in 4 sections, but not *equal* portions and thus cannot be considered fourths.

Facilitating the Math Congress

Tech tip:

You might take pictures of students' work using a cell or iPad and project them onto a whiteboard or smart board. When different ideas come up in discussions, you can circle issues under discussion and revisions can be drawn without having to mark on the student's work. Apps such as *Adobe Sketch* or *Explain Everything* can be useful tools.

Inside One Classroom: a portion of the congress

Tammie (teacher): What a great gallery walk we had! This was a hard challenge and I saw so many wonderful little cities and posters about important ideas! Several of you noticed that all the faces of the buildings are rectangles no matter what shape the footprint is, so let's start by talking about that idea. Isabella, would you and Maria come up and share what you wrote about?

Isabella: We noticed that all the sides of the buildings are like rectangles. We made this building on a triangle bottom and it had 3 sides. But the sides are all rectangles. And this one we made with

Author's notes

Tammie chooses to start the congress with a discussion of how the faces of the buildings are all rectangles no matter what shape the footprints are. Starting the congress with this piece of work

the hexagon. It has 6 sides and the building had 6 sides. **Tammie:** Wow! Put your hand up if you understand what Isabella and Maria mean? (Lots of hands go up). Let's call the "sides" of the buildings "faces," ok? That's what mathematicians call them. The hexagon has 6 sides, and the hexagonal prism—that's the shape of the building you made—has 6 rectangular faces. Do you want to add to that, Maria? **Maria:** The number of sides on the bottom shape is the same as the number of sides of the building. See..., the rectangle part of the net goes around it. When we did the rhombus, it had 4 equal sides and then there were 4 equal faces around the building. And they were rectangles, too. All the sides of all the buildings are rectangles. **Tammie:** Josiah? **Josiah:** I know why. When you fold the rectangle, it is a straight line. We are just making smaller rectangles.	*will involve everyone and will provide an entrée into a discussion on the relationship of the number of sides of the polygon to the number of sections needed to be made with the folding of the rectangle. This move supports the development of relational thinking -looking for structure and regularity—an important standard of mathematical practice. A conversation like this will be beneficial for all.*
Tammie: Annie, you and Ella talked about that, too. Just like what Josiah said. Come up with your poster and add on to what Josiah just said. **Annie:** We saw that the folding was like making fractions. Like Josiah said, the folding just made 4 smaller rectangles. For the building with a square bottom we folded the rectangle in half, and then half again. That gave us 4 equal pieces for the faces. Ms. Hullivan said we had made fractions: ¼ + ¼ + ¼ + ¼ (pointing to each face). **Kacy:** Oh, I get it! That's cool. You made 4 smaller rectangles out of the bigger one and they are all equal because the square has 4 equal sides!	*Annie and Ella have explored fractions and, when Tammie conferred with them, she had introduced the fraction notation.*
Tammie: It is cool, isn't it...how different shapes when joined are related? We can tell so much by looking for relationships. And if these four faces are each ¼, then the whole rectangle that we folded is 4/4. (*Tammie writes the notation*). This just means that if you have 4 fourths you have the whole thing.	*Note how Tammie refers to relationships. This models another mathematical practice—looking for structure and regularity.*

Matthew and Wyatt, you noticed some relationships, too. You put 3 orange squares together and made a rectangle base and you also did a trapezoid. Those shapes made 4 rectangular faces, too, but they weren't fourths, right? Come tell us what happened. What did you notice? **Matthew**: The rectangle had 4 sides, so we got 4 smaller rectangles. But they weren't all the same size. Two were skinny, and 2 were much wider. **Tammie**: Oh, my goodness! Four rectangles but not fourths because they aren't the same size! Turn and talk to an elbow partner about this. (*After a few minutes of pair talk)* Wyatt? **Wyatt:** At first, we thought we had made a mistake! But then we saw why. These two sides are longer because we used 3 squares for the basement. This side is 1, then 3, then 1, then 3.	*Now the conversation shifts to the trapezoid and non-square rectangles. Both polygons are also quadrilaterals, but the lengths of the sides are not all equal and therefore the lateral faces of the prisms will not all be equal, even though they will still be rectangular.*
Sasha: Hey, I just noticed another relationship. I know what is going to happen with the trapezoid! There will be 4 rectangle sides of the building, because the trapezoid has 4 sides, too, but the rectangles won't be fourths either, because one side of the trapezoid is really long. I think it will be thirds and then one big piece. **Tammie***: (Holding up the big rectangle that was folded.)* Well, actually..., these three are 3 equal pieces, nice noticing! But are they thirds? Is the whole rectangle then 3 thirds? (*Now everyone looks puzzled.)* Turn and talk about this.	*Sasha brings up a common misconception about fractions. When children are introduced to fractions with a part/parts model they often focus on the equivalence of the parts and lose sight of what the whole is.*

Reflections on the Day

Today, students had the opportunity to work in small peer review groups to clarify and discuss some of the emerging big ideas they are constructing about geometric shapes. As students prepared their posters and participated in the gallery walk and subsequent congress, they explored further the properties of two-dimensional shapes and how these affected the properties of the resulting prisms they are making. They also explored and discussed some early notions about fractions and were introduced to the importance of determining the whole. The notation of 3/3 and 4/4 for the whole was introduced and the big idea that the whole matters may have even arisen in the discussion as it did in the field test classroom depicted in the dialogue box at the end. Tomorrow students will add arrays to their city models as they make rectangular patios with tiles. Note how a foundation is being laid for topics your students will continue to explore in years to come.

DAY FOUR

EXPLORING TILED ARRAYS

Materials Needed

- Quick Image Shapes (Appendix E)
- City Models (student work from the prior days)
- Math Journals
- Pencils
- ¼ inch-grid paper (2-3 sheets per pair of students)
- Scissors
- Drawing paper
- Glue sticks

The day begins again with a minilesson on analyzing and sorting polygons by their properties. Then a context of making small rectangular patios out of grid paper for the little city is introduced. Students cut out various-sized rectangular arrays out of grid paper and determine how many square tiles will be needed for each and what the cost will be at $2 a tile.

Day Four Outline

Minilesson: Quick Images

❖ Show one quick image from Appendix E at a time and invite students to share the properties they saw.

❖ Invite discussion on the properties and sort each image by the number of sides and corners as you go.

❖ At the end of the minilesson you should have only 2 groups. Label them pentagons and hexagons and provide discussion on how pentagons are 5-sided closed figures and hexagons are 6-sided closed figures. The lengths of the sides don't have to be the same.

Developing the Context

❖ Invite students to talk about tiled patios they have seen in backyards or in cities.

❖ Ask students to work in pairs, cutting out several small rectangles of various sizes from grid paper, determining how many squares in each, and what the cost of the tiles will be for each.

Supporting the Investigation

❖ Confer as students work.

Facilitating a Math Congress

❖ Facilitate a discussion on strategies used to determine the number of squares in the patios and the cost of the tiles, focusing conversation on how it's easy to skip squares when counting by ones. Rows and columns can be helpful to notice and use as then one can skipcount or use repeated addition.

Minilesson: Quick Images

Gather the children around you in a meeting area. Explain that you will be doing another "quick images" minilesson. Draw two circles labeled by number of sides and corners. The first circle should say 5 sides and 5 corners; the second, 6 sides and 6 corners. Show one card at a time from Appendix E, moving it from your right to your left, then behind your back. With each card ask, *"What did you see and how many sides and corners does it have?"* After discussion on the shape seen ask students which circle the shape goes in. Allow students to name the shape if they know it, but don't push names at this point. Just sort the shapes by their properties. You will be introducing the terms pentagons and hexagons once all shapes have been sorted.

Show each image one at a time for a few seconds and then remove it. After each quick image ask children how many sides and corners the shape had and when all agree place it in the appropriate circle. When all shapes have been shown and sorted name the two categories: pentagons and hexagons. Explain that pentagons are 5-sided closed shapes, and hexagons are 6-sided closed shapes. Allow discussion on how the shapes don't have to look alike; when determining the name of the shape, only the properties matter.

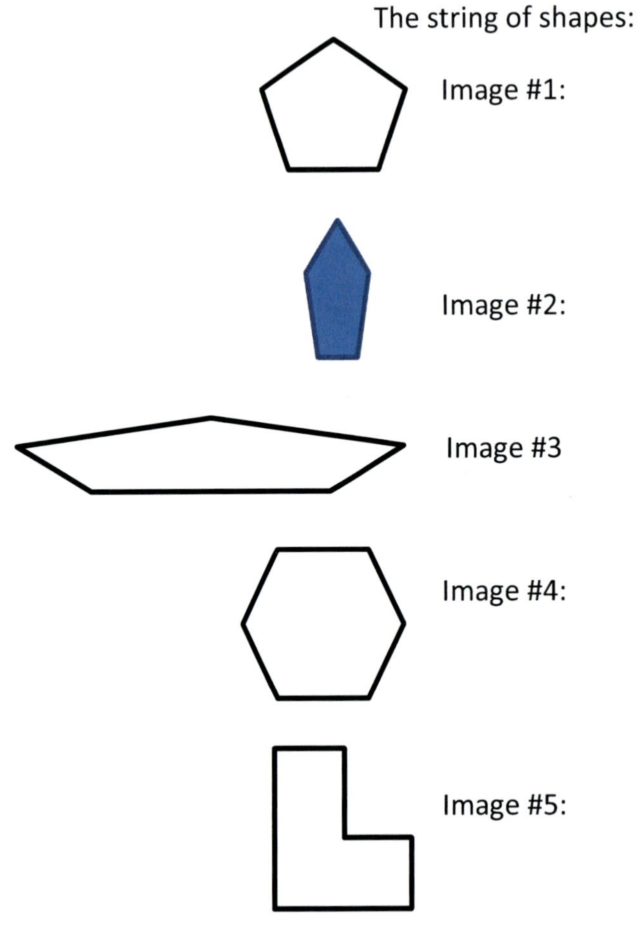

Image #6:

Developing the Context

Begin developing the context by inviting students to discuss what they know about patios in backyards, attached to apartment buildings, or perhaps even in courtyards or city parks.

> **Tech Note:**
>
> **If you google "tiled patio images" you will likely find several images you can use to introduce the context. Choose images that show rectangular arrays.**

Explain that today patios of various sizes will be designed and cut out for the little cities. They won't be added to the models yet though. First, as city planners, students will need to make notes on the number of square tiles to buy and the cost. Each tile costs $2.

Once students understand the goal of the day's task, formulate pairs, provide each with grid paper, drawing paper, glue sticks and scissors.

Supporting the Investigation

As students work, move around the room and confer as needed to support and challenge. As students work to determine the number of squares, you will likely see a variety of strategies:

- Many will count by ones and will not make use of rows and columns. They may count across a row and then work down a side, then across the bottom and up the left side using a sort of picture frame strategy. They may even count the squares in the corners twice. As you confer with these students, ask them if there might be a way to organize their work so they can remember which squares they have already counted. Ask them if they know how many squares are in one row and if that will help them with the next row.
- Some students may count by ones but make use of rows (or columns) as an organizational tool. Suggest that if they know how many squares are in one row, they can use repeated addition or skipcounting strategies.

- Some students may use repeated addition or skipcounting at the start but be challenged by it depending on their fluency with adding the numbers. Wonder aloud if it might be helpful to combine groups to make the repeated addition easier.
- Some students may partition the array and work section by section. Wonder aloud if the sections were equal (for example cut into halves or fourths), if that might make figuring out the total easier since they would then only have either 2 or 4 groups to add. Note whether they realize when they partition the array into halves that the two halves have the same number of squares. Focus conversation on this if they don't.
- Depending on when in the year you use this unit and if you have already used Groceries, Stamps, and Measuring Strips (to introduce early multiplication), a few students might use partial products.
- Once students determine the number of tiles and begin working on the cost, do they realize they can just double the answer to get the cost of tiles, or do they try to recount all over again, this time by twos?

Facilitating the Math Congress

Use your congress to discuss the strategies used. This is a nice congress to scaffold progressively moving from counting by ones, to skipcounting, to repeated addition and regrouping strategies. When discussing strategies for finding the cost of the tiles, if you have students who used doubling and students who have counted by twos, this is a nice moment to focus on how both strategies work and why (2 x a = a x 2). The commutative property of multiplication is a big idea here.

Reflections on the Day

Students explored several big ideas today about arrays. Although most of the strategies used to determine the number of tiles may have been counting by ones, as they worked with the arrays many may have begun to understand how arrays are comprised of rows and columns. This by itself is a big idea and should be celebrated. Understanding that a square is in a row and a column simultaneously requires a great deal of cognitive reorganization for students, and this will serve them well when they begin to work with arrays for multiplication in later grades. Don't forget to assess. Save the work from each day, take some pictures, and make note of the conversations you hear. Highlight the growth you see on the landscape using the landscape graphics in the Overview, or use our assessment app: www.NewPerspectivesOnAssessment.com.

DAY FIVE

PARTITIONING PATIOS FAIRLY

Materials Needed

City Models (student work from the prior days)

Math Journals

Pencils

Four Patio Designs (Appendix F)

Today students are told a story about neighbors in a few apartment buildings who want to divide their patio up into equal areas so they will each have a private patio. Students work to determine if the subdivisions are equal or not. The partitions look different. Do shapes need to look alike to be equivalent? The patios are then added to the city models and the models are all placed together to make one large city. In the center, students can add blank paper for a park and circles if they wish for flower beds. The circles can be divided into fourths with four different colors of flowers shown. The day ends with journal writing and the production of a learning scroll that shows evidence of the progression of learning throughout the unit.

Day Five Outline

Developing the Context

❖ Show the designs of patio divisions on Appendix F and explain that some neighbors want to divide their patios up into 4 equal sections so that they each have a private patio.

❖ Ask students to work in pairs examining the four plans and determining if the divisions have produced equal areas and are therefore fourths.

Supporting the Investigation

❖ Confer as students work encouraging them to prove that the parts are all equal and that the parts do not need to look alike to be equivalent.

Facilitating Math Congress

❖ Focus congress on a discussion of strategies that prove: fourths are equal, ½ of ½ =1/4, the whole is 4/4, and parts do not have to congruent to be equal. End the congress with the making of a learning scroll that shows the learning over the 5 days of the unit.

Developing the Context

Display Appendix F and explain that some neighbors decided to divide their patio up into 4 equal spaces so they could each have a private space. They drew some possible designs and now they are arguing about whether their patios have equal space. Do they all really have ¼ each?

Once students understand the goal of the day's task, formulate pairs, provide each pair with a copy of Appendix F, and send them off to determine if the partitioning in each plan was fair and to develop an argument to convince others they are right.

Supporting the Investigation

Be prepared with this activity to find several students who adamantly state the partitioning is not equal. Usually they have used a counting strategy and miscounted. See Figure 8.

Figure 8: Counting

Other students will cut out the sections and establish congruency by overlaying the pieces. Some may work to prove that in all cases the patios have been partitioned into halves first and then partitioned again into halves. See Figure 9.

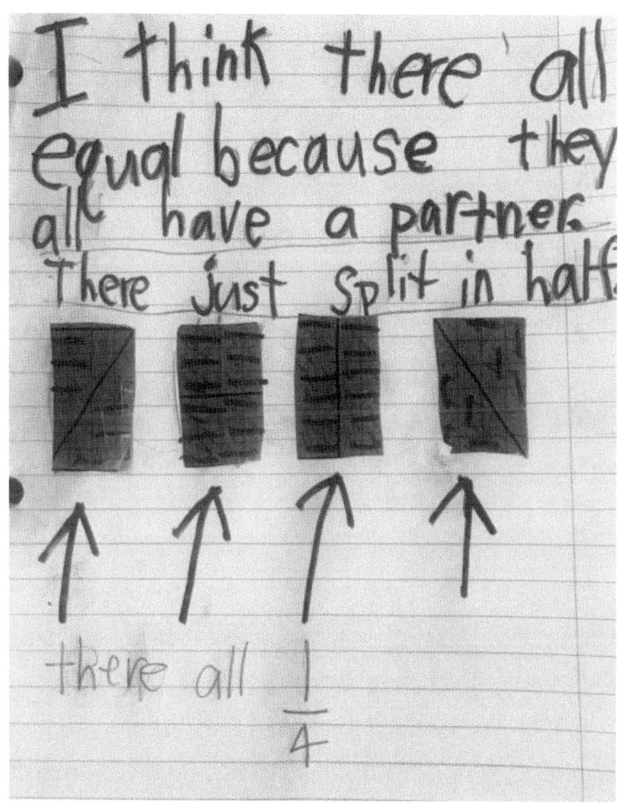

Figure 9: Cutting

Facilitating a Congress

The congress will likely be a spirited one with students disagreeing if some have counted and gotten different numbers. It is helpful to structure the discussion on one patio design at a time, starting with the easiest (design #2), where the fourths are easily seen as congruent. Then move to Design #1. Allow a student who has miscounted and thinks the triangular sections are not equal (for example, as shown in Figure 8) to share, and then invite a student who has cut the sections out to prove the pieces are congruent (for example, as shown in Figure 9). Laying the pieces on top of one another should be enough to establish equality and to label each section ¼ with the whole being 4/4. If the triangles are each ¼, then the bottom half of Design #3 must be ½. If you have a student who has folded (or cut) each of the patios in half, focus the conversation on this strategy and encourage students to see how the halves in each case have been halved again.

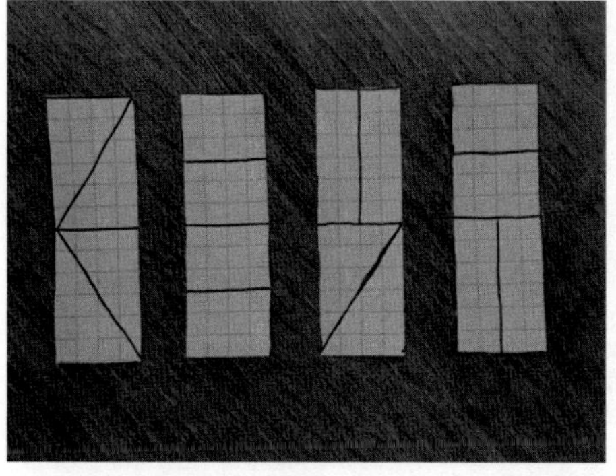

At the end of the congress, turn the conversation to a discussion of all the learning that has happened during the implementation of the unit. Invite students to talk about insights they had along the way. Perhaps some students didn't realize that shapes could look different but still have the same name—that all 3-sided shapes with 3 angles are triangles no matter what they look like. Perhaps students will talk about how turning 2-D polygons in 3-D prisms created surprises and discoveries about how the sides of the buildings, no matter the footprint, were all rectangles. Others may share how they now have new insights about rows and columns in arrays, and thus new strategies for determining how many squares there are in an array. Lastly, foster discussion on how fractions were introduced, how ½ of ½ is ¼, how fractional pieces don't have to look alike to be equal, and how the whole can be represented as 3/3 or 4/4, etc. Use this discussion to make a learning scroll.

A learning scroll is a class display—a sort of "socio-historical" wall—documenting the progression of the unit, children's questions, the important ideas constructed over the past week, samples of students' work, and descriptions of their strategies and ideas, including anecdotes where appropriate of how students' thinking changed over time. It is a document of the progression and emergence of learning over time. By making this display available, you allow your students to revisit and reflect on all the wonderful ideas and strategies that emerged as they worked throughout the unit. Developmentally, second graders will need you to scaffold some of this reflection work, but they will also be able to partner in identifying and describing their thoughts and strategies. An example of the one produced in the field testing of the unit is below.

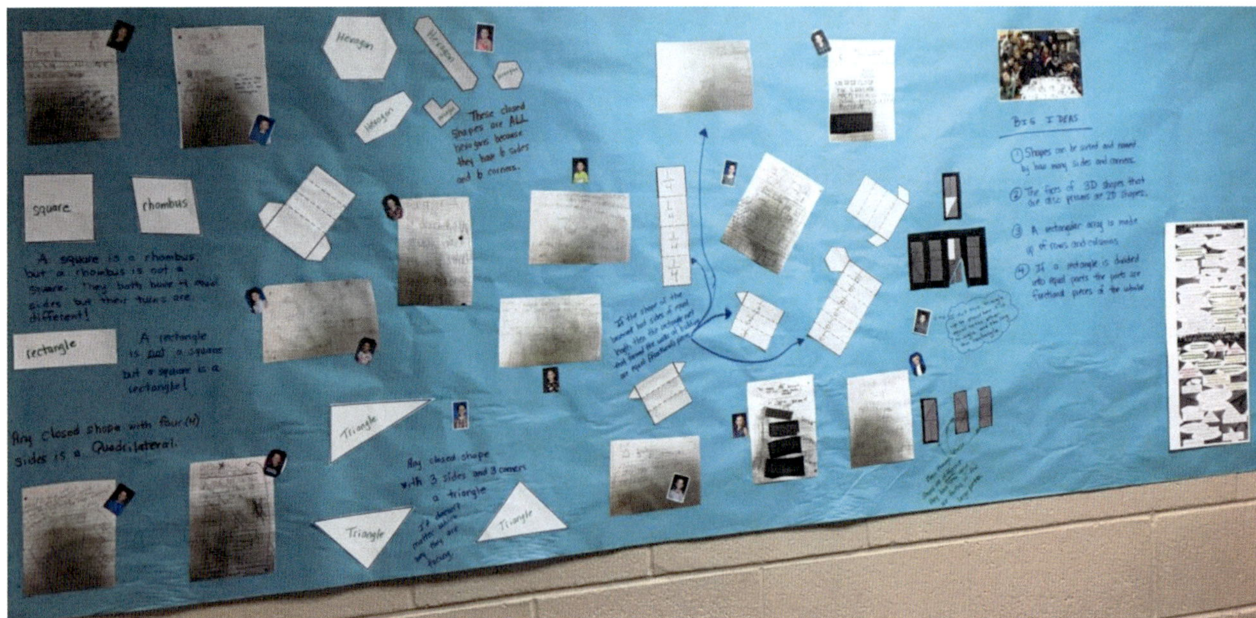

In preparation for today's work, use a roll of chart paper and cut out a long length enough to cover a bulletin board or a display area in a hallway. Curl and staple the two ends, making a small roll on each end like a scroll. Staple or tape the scroll to the area to be covered. Selectively pick key pieces of children's work from the course of the unit and include these on a pathway from left to right, leaving plenty of blank space for anecdotes and explanations. You can also include pictures of the students and use a speech bubble to show insights they had along the way, or ideas they had that were disproved.

You may want to provide templates with empty speech bubbles with prompts like "At first I thought..." "Then I realized..." and "A good strategy was..." Attach these student explanations to the learning scroll. Wherever you can, show the developmental emergence of ideas from the landscape in the Overview. Display the scroll somewhere that students (and hopefully also the wider school community) will be able to revisit and reflect on the learning in the weeks to come.

Reflection on the Unit

"Once upon a time there was a sensible **straight line** *who was hopelessly in love with a* **dot**. *'You're the beginning and the end, the hub, the core and the quintessence,' he told her tenderly, but the frivolous dot wasn't a bit interested, for she only had eyes for a wild and unkempt squiggle who never seemed to have anything on his mind at all. All of the line's romantic dreams were in vain, until he discovered......angles! Now, with newfound self-expression, he can be anything he wants to be—a square, a triangle, a parallelogram. And, that's just the beginning!"*

Norton Juster

Norton Juster is an architect and planner, professor emeritus of design at Hampshire College, and the author of several highly acclaimed children's books, including *The Dot and the Line*, which was made into an Academy Award-winning animated film. Over the course of this unit, your students have been engaged in the studying and exploring of geometry. They worked as city planners and architects designing a little city, drawing and categorizing polygons by their properties, and transforming these 2-D shapes into 3-D prisms as models for their buildings.

Now that the unit has ended, you might want to get a copy of the book *The Dot and the Line* and read it to your children. Take a photo of the city your community of learners made to remind them of all the work they did: first, with lines and dots as they outlined polygonal footprints for their buildings, and then with the folding of nets to make prisms to model the buildings in three dimensions. The beauty of their transformations, their surprises, and the ultimate joys of creating will stay with them for a long time, if not forever. Capture the memories.

LITTLE
CITIES

Appendix A

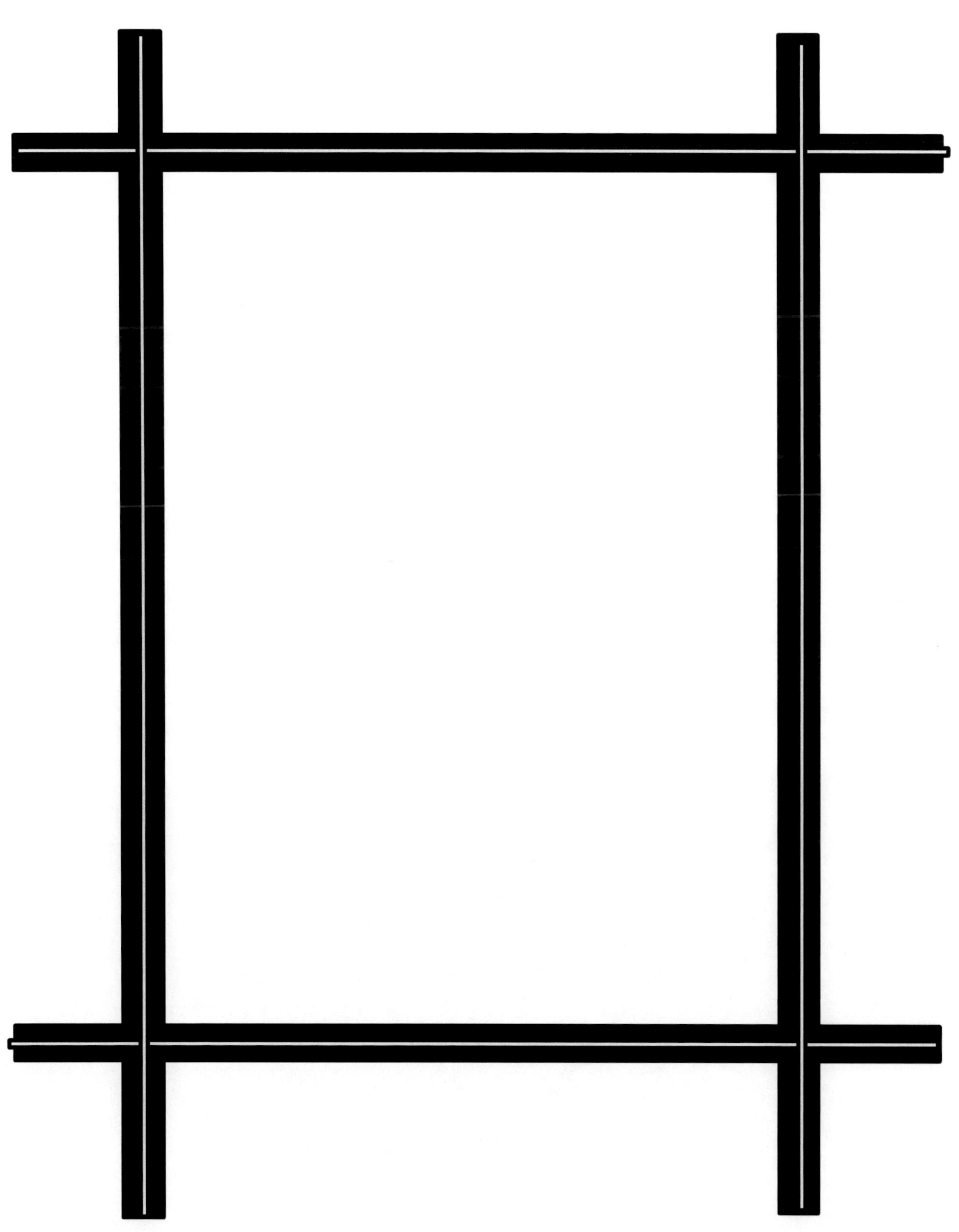

Appendix B (1 of 4)

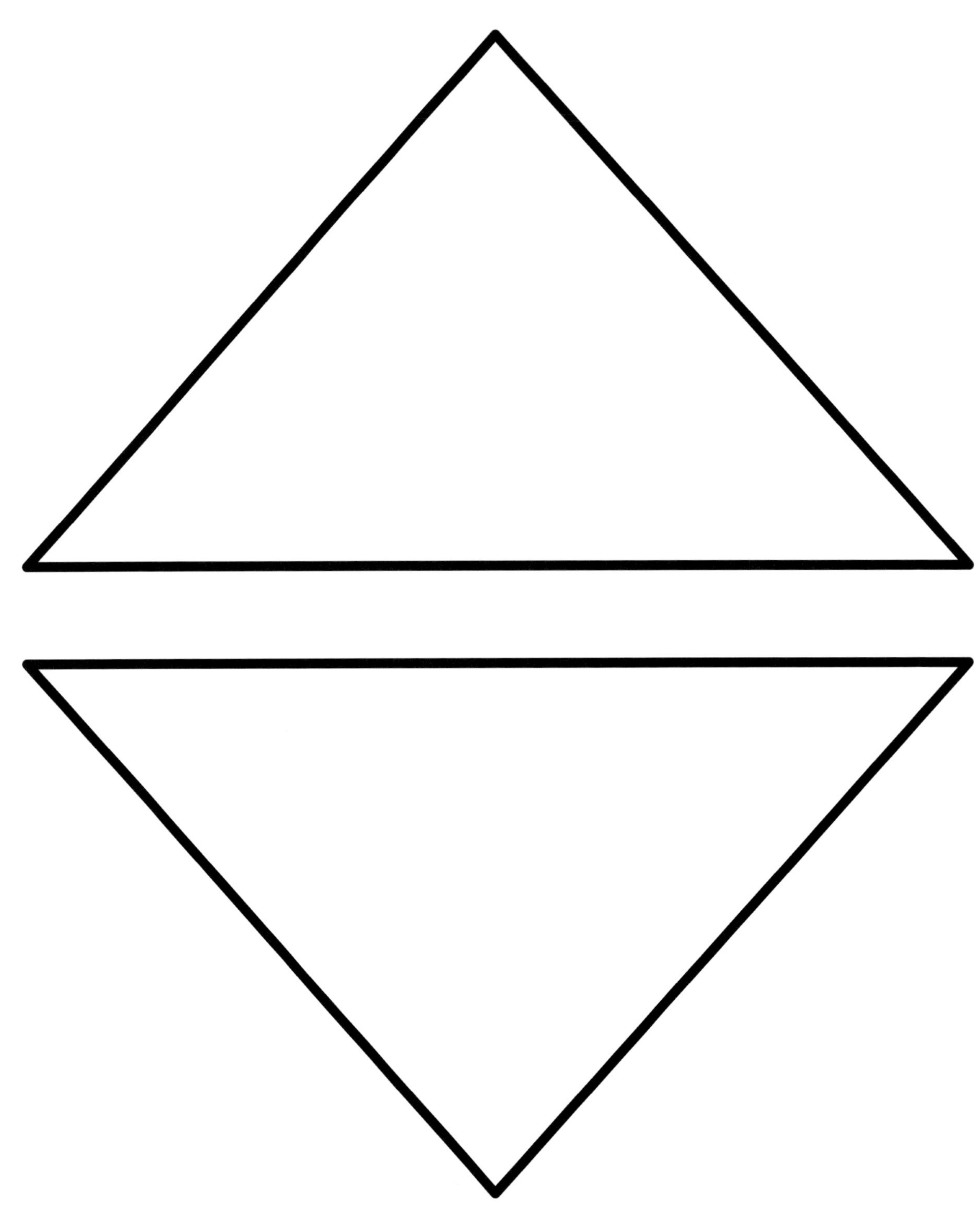

Appendix B (2 of 4)

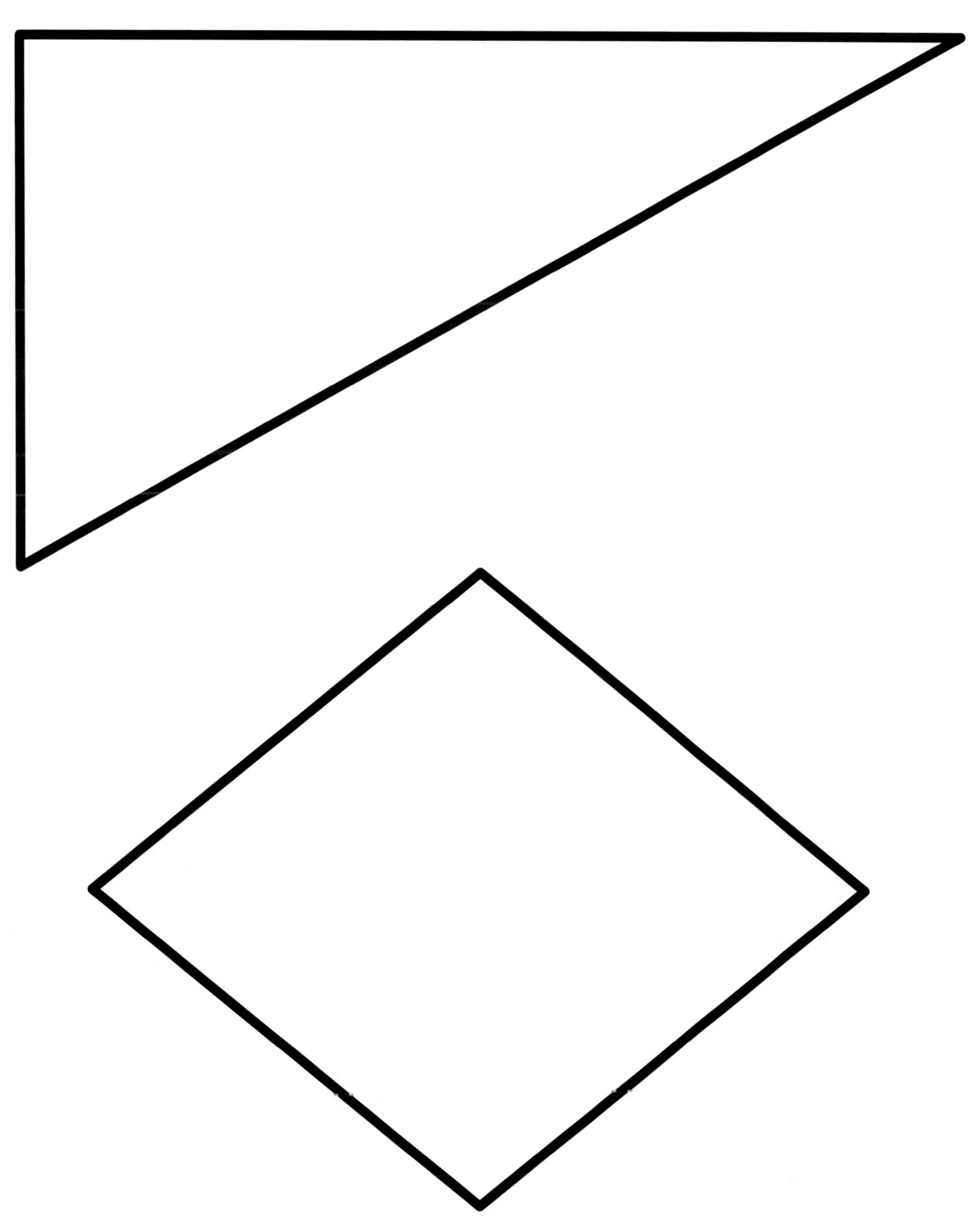

Appendix B (3 of 4)

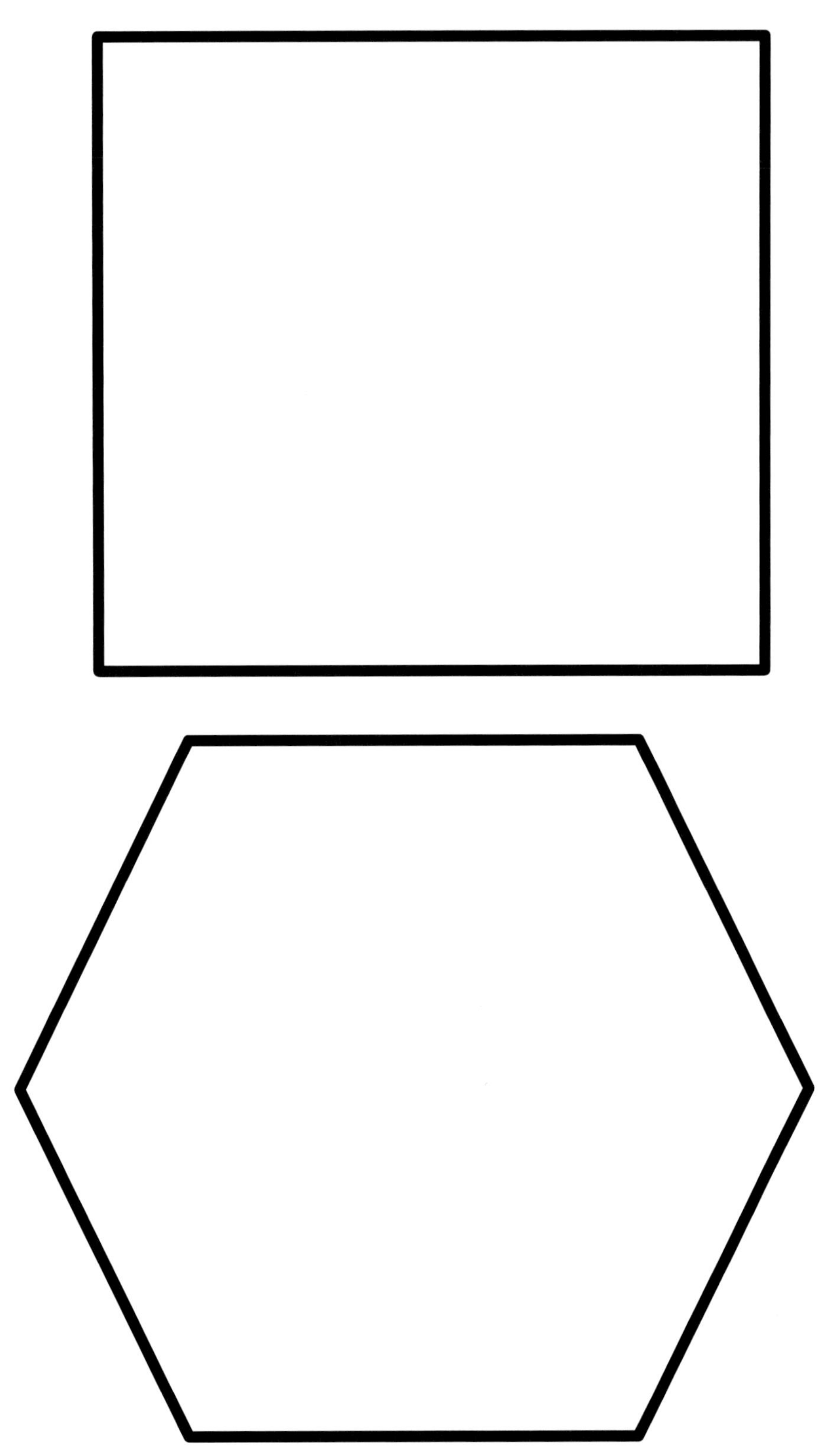

Appendix B (4 of 4)

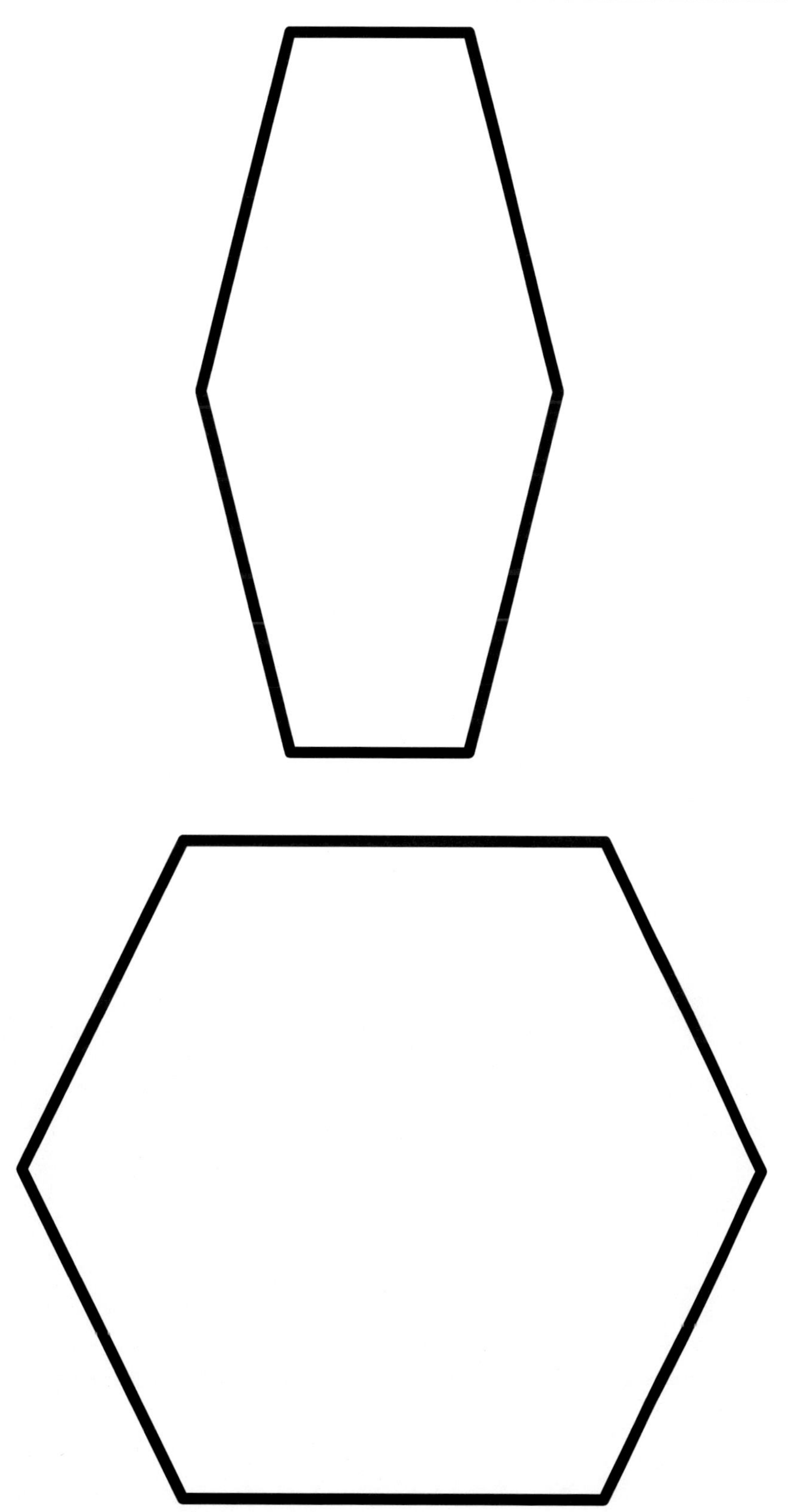

Appendix C (1 of 3)

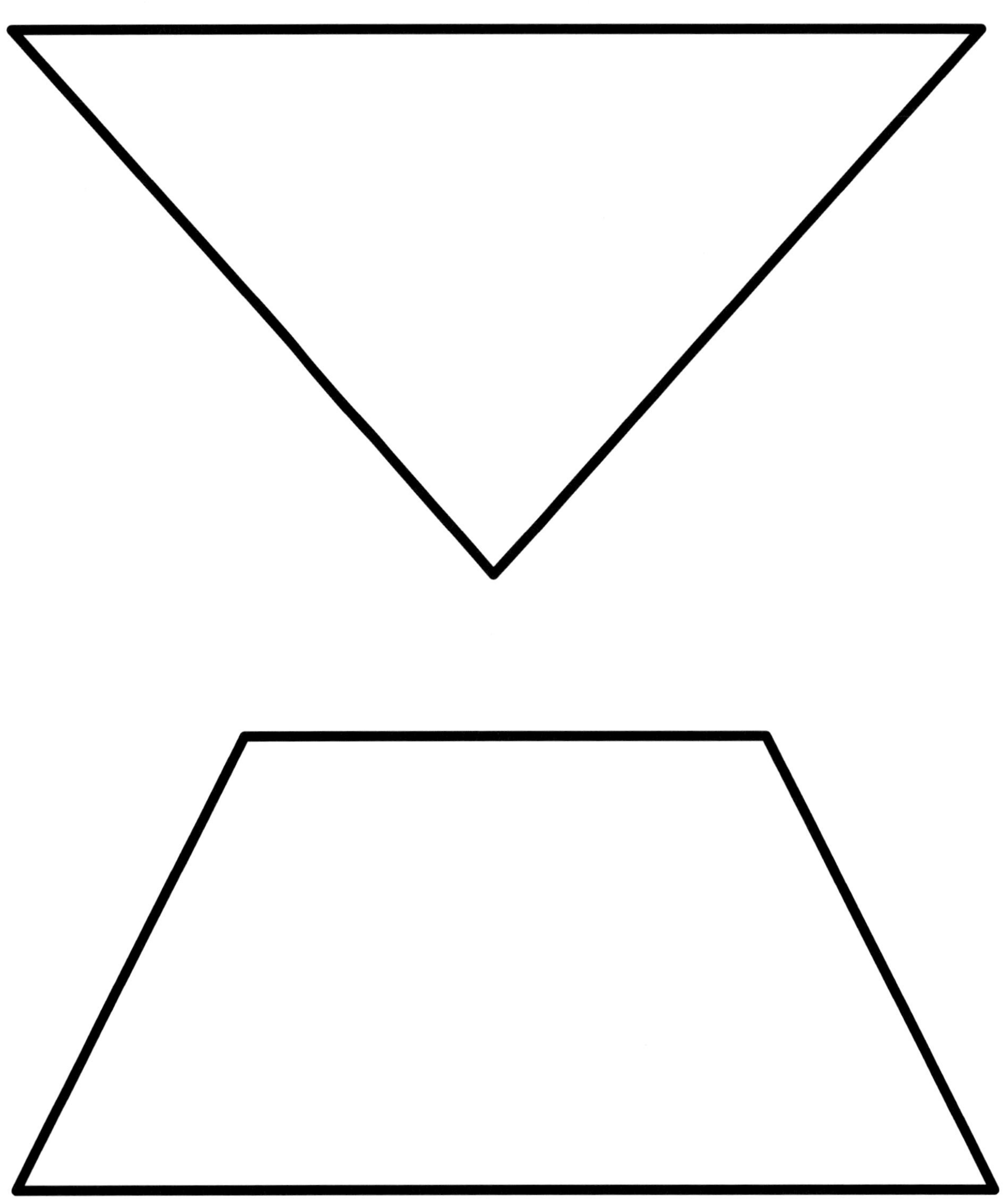

Appendix C (2 of 3)

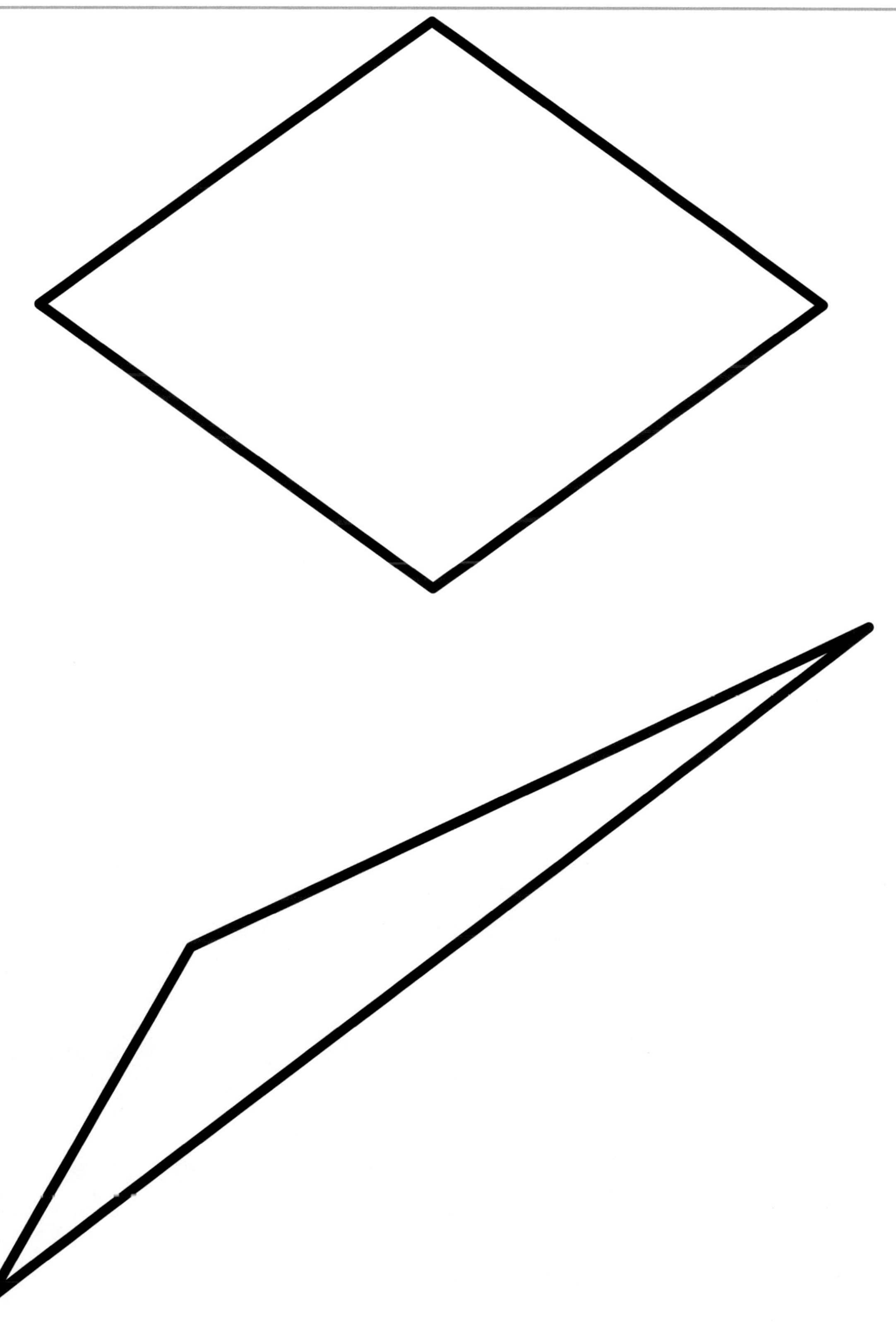

Appendix C (3 of 3)

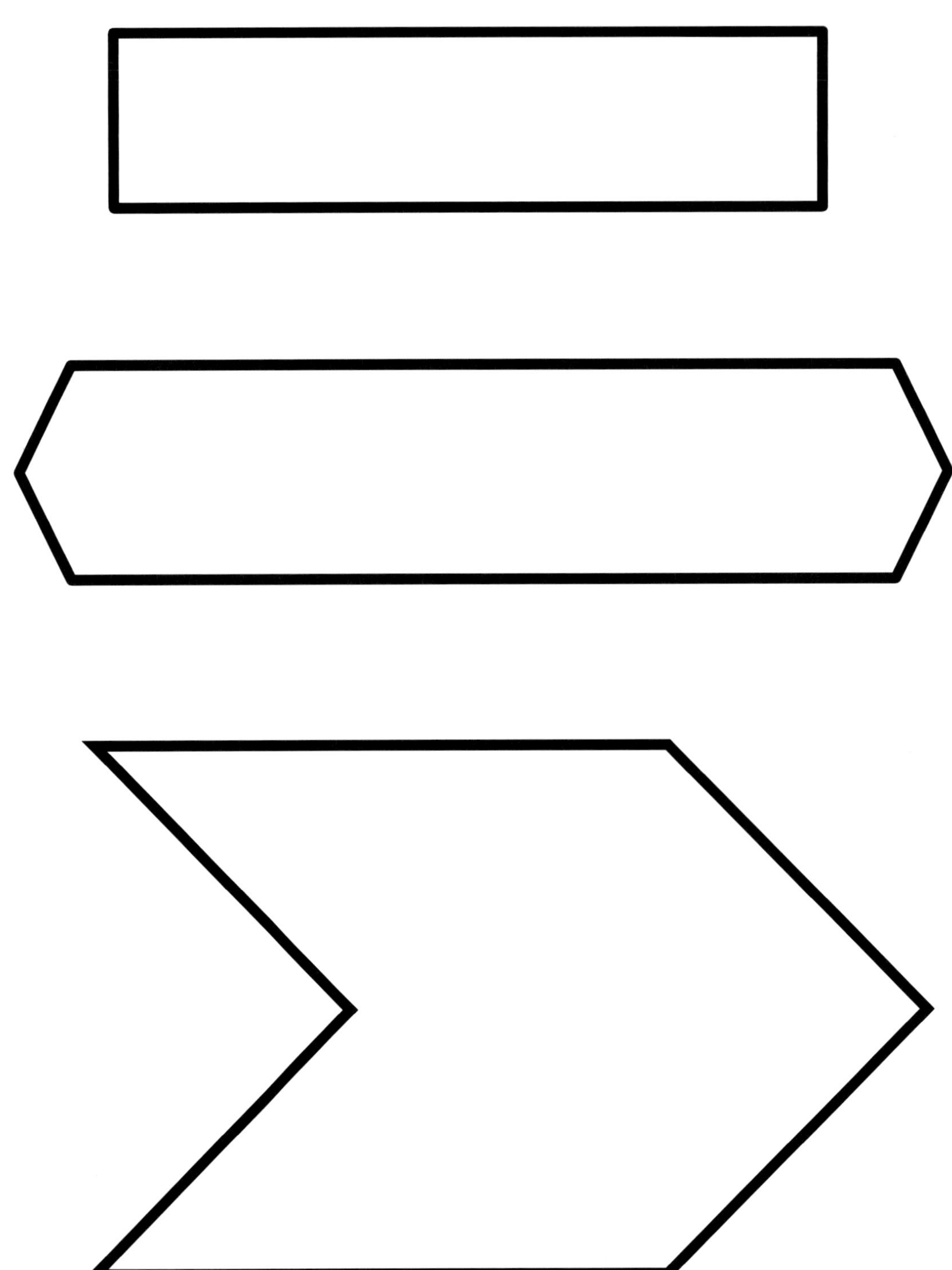

Appendix D (8 nets)

The nets follow on pages 58-63. Because of the needed sizes to ensure the proper fit around the pattern blocks, each page had to printed without the title of the Appendix.

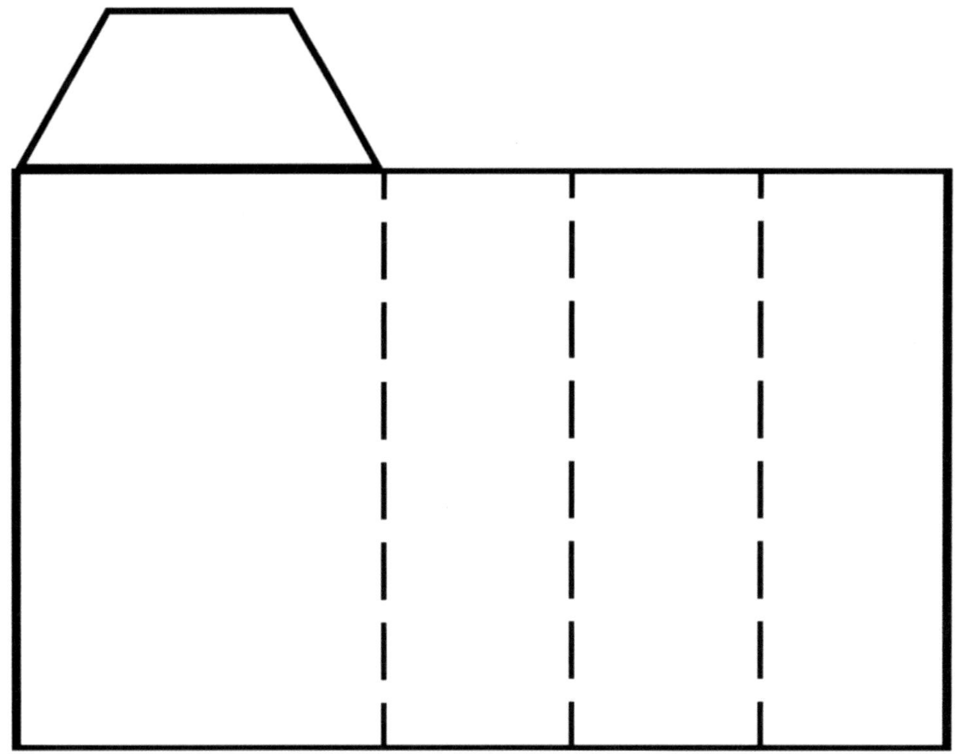

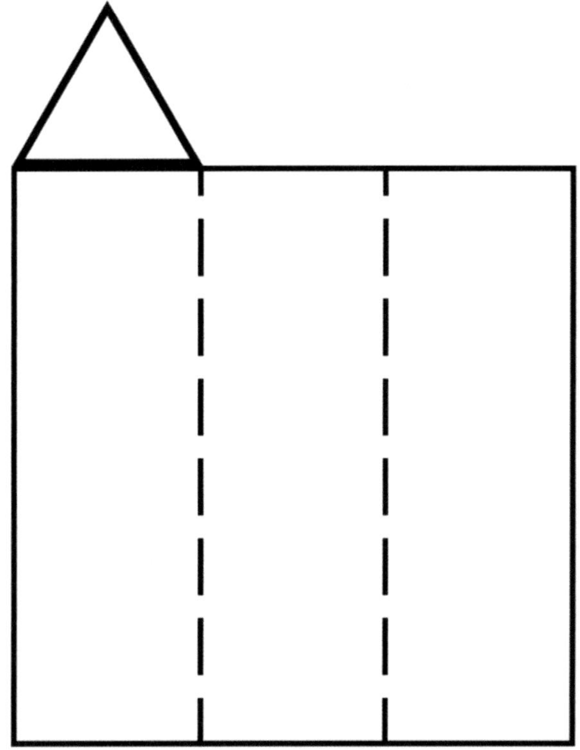

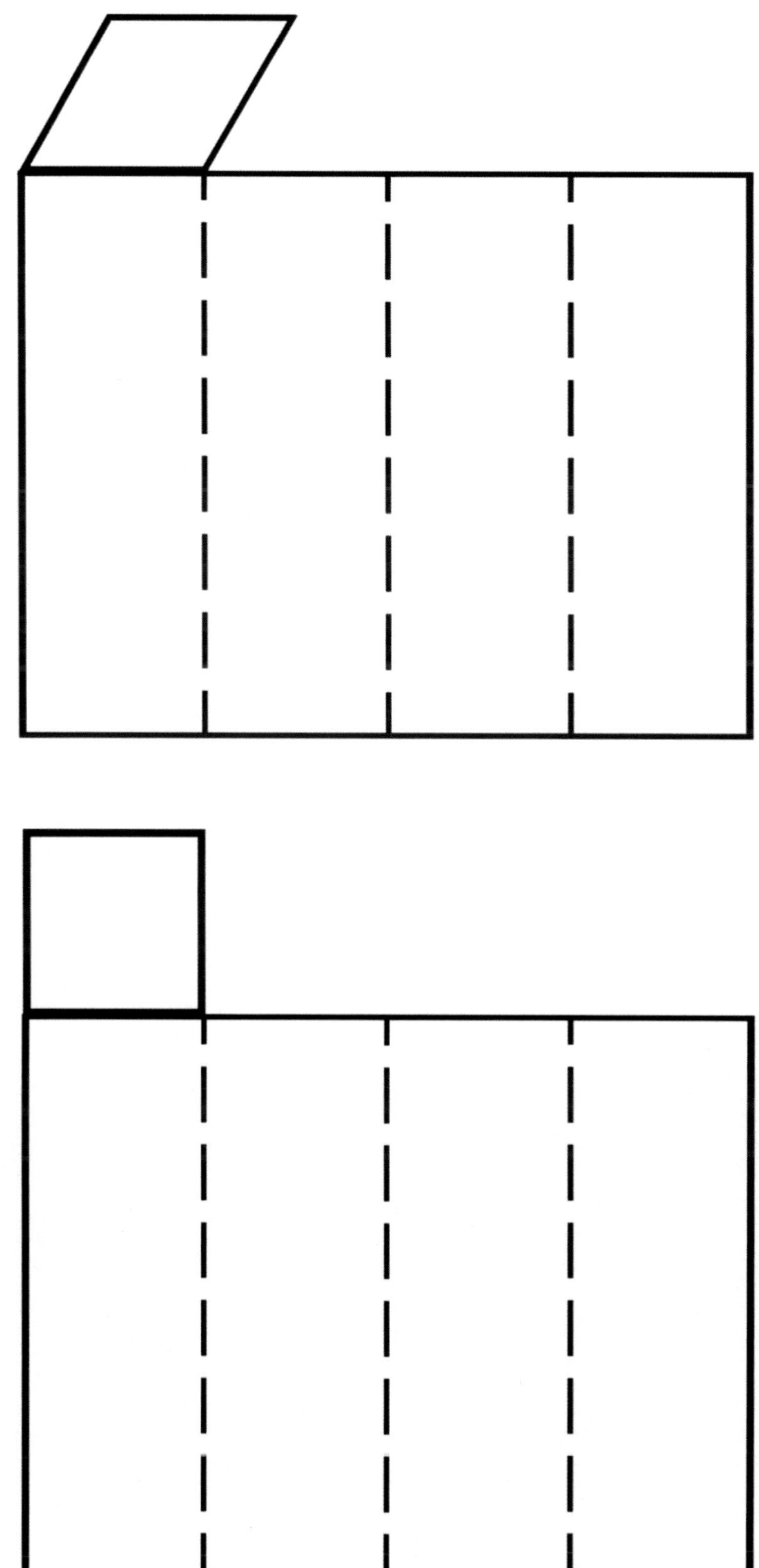

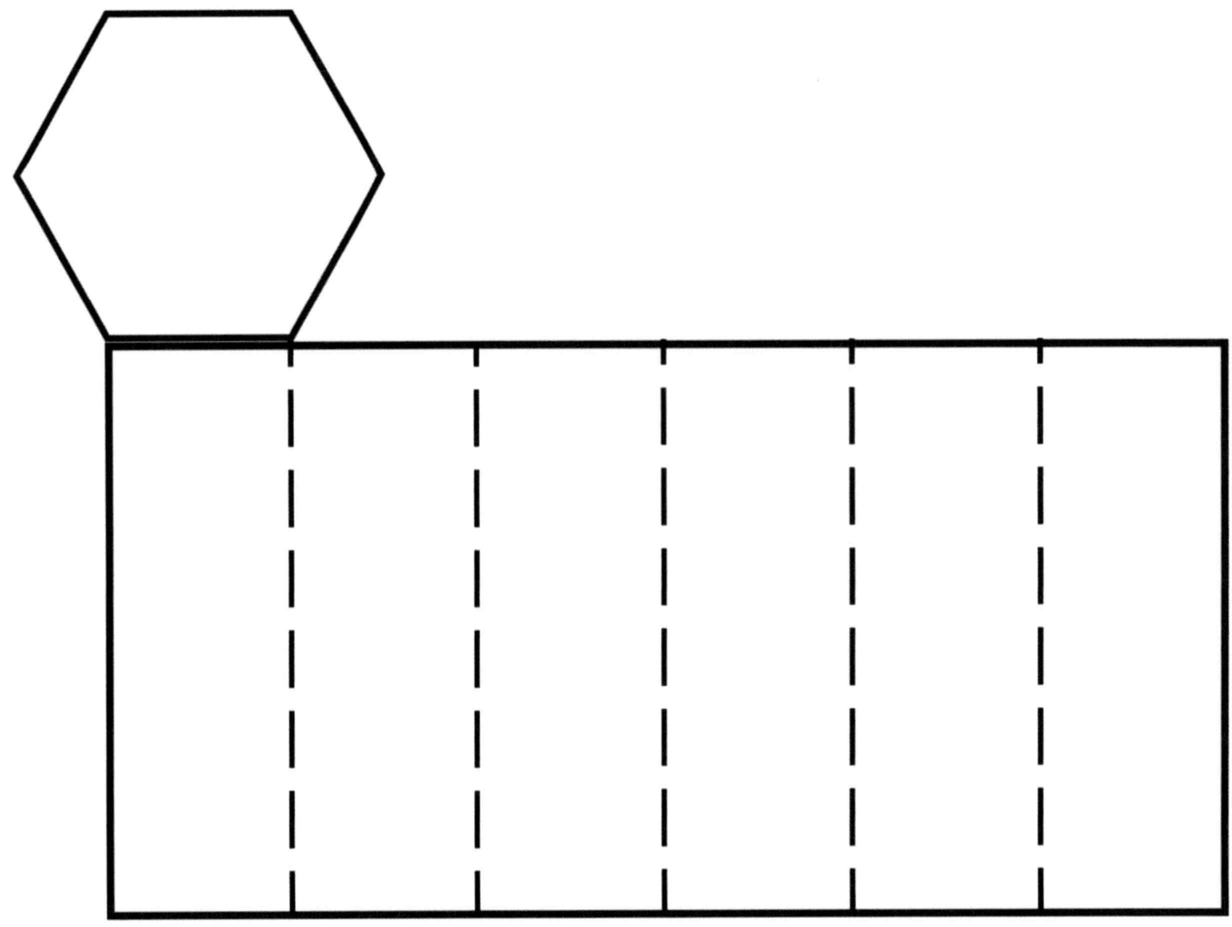

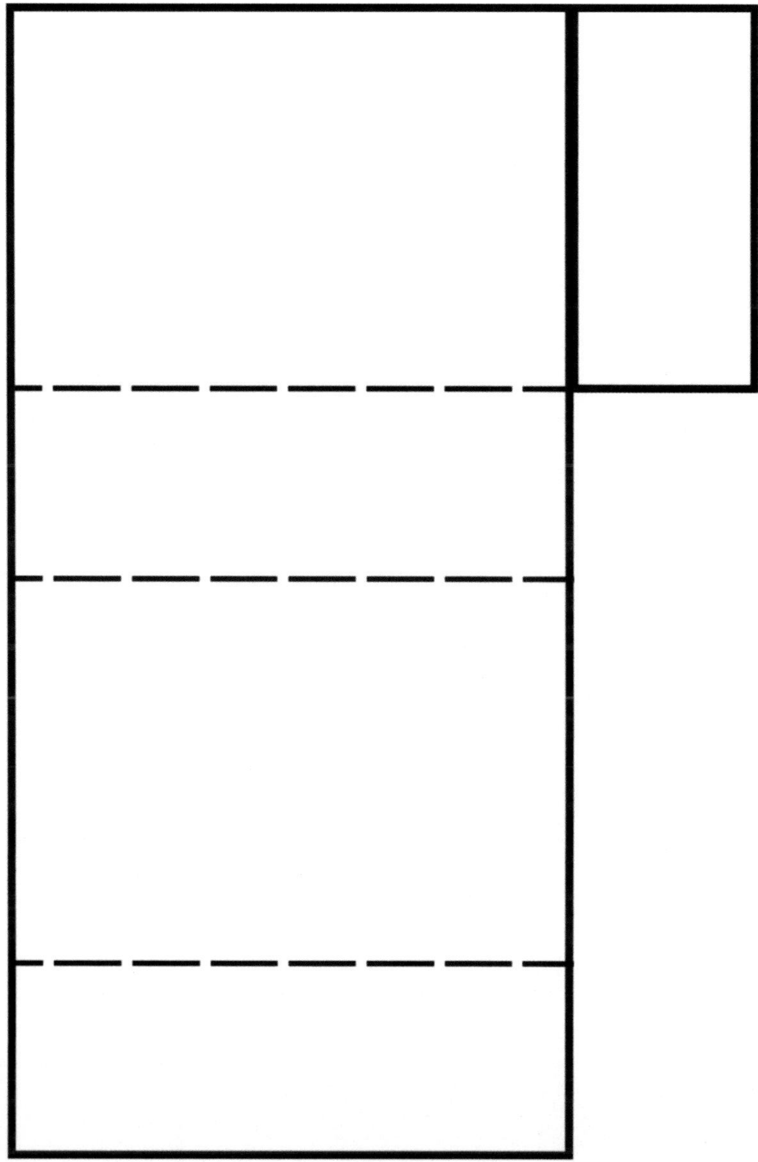

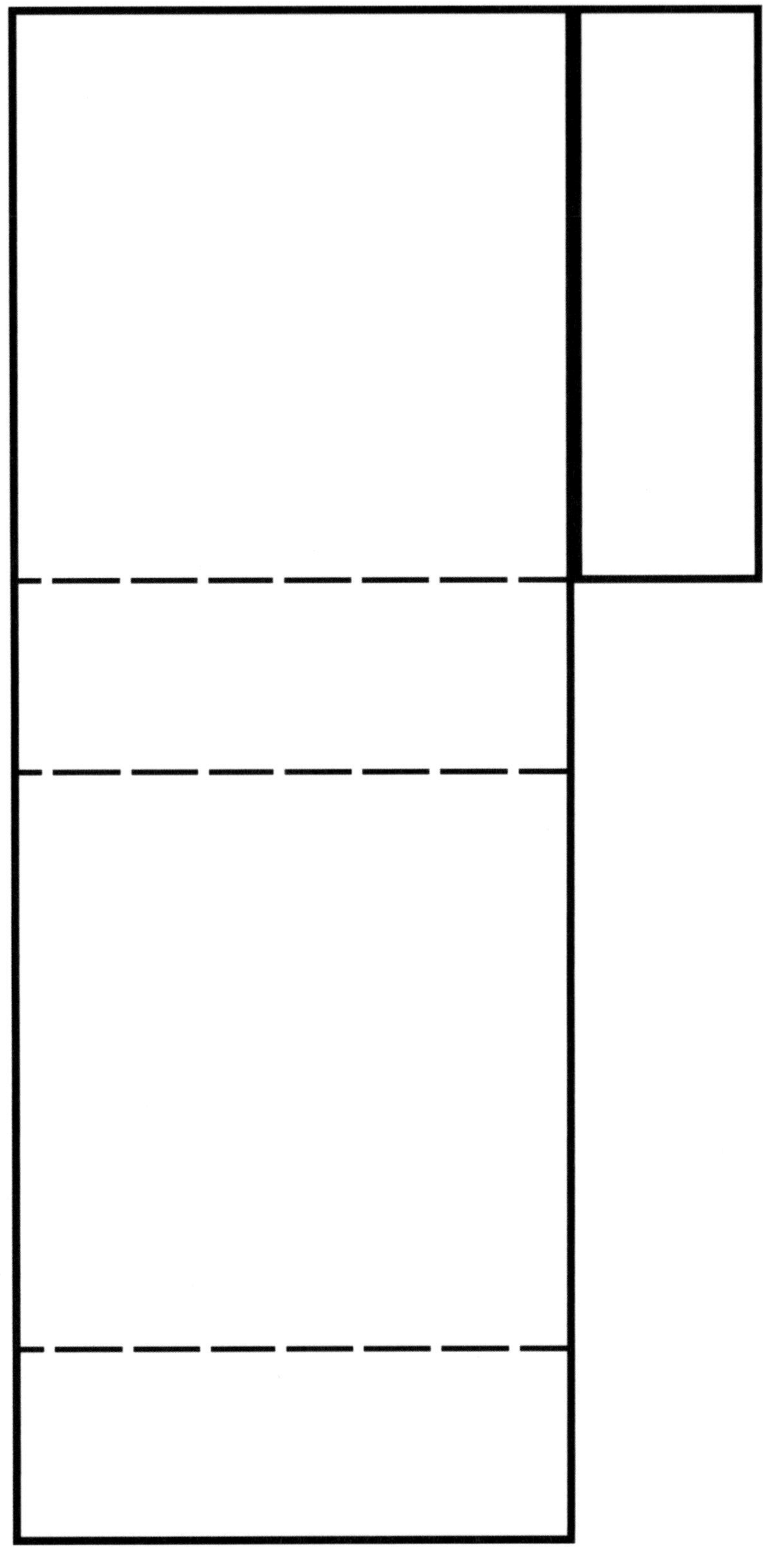

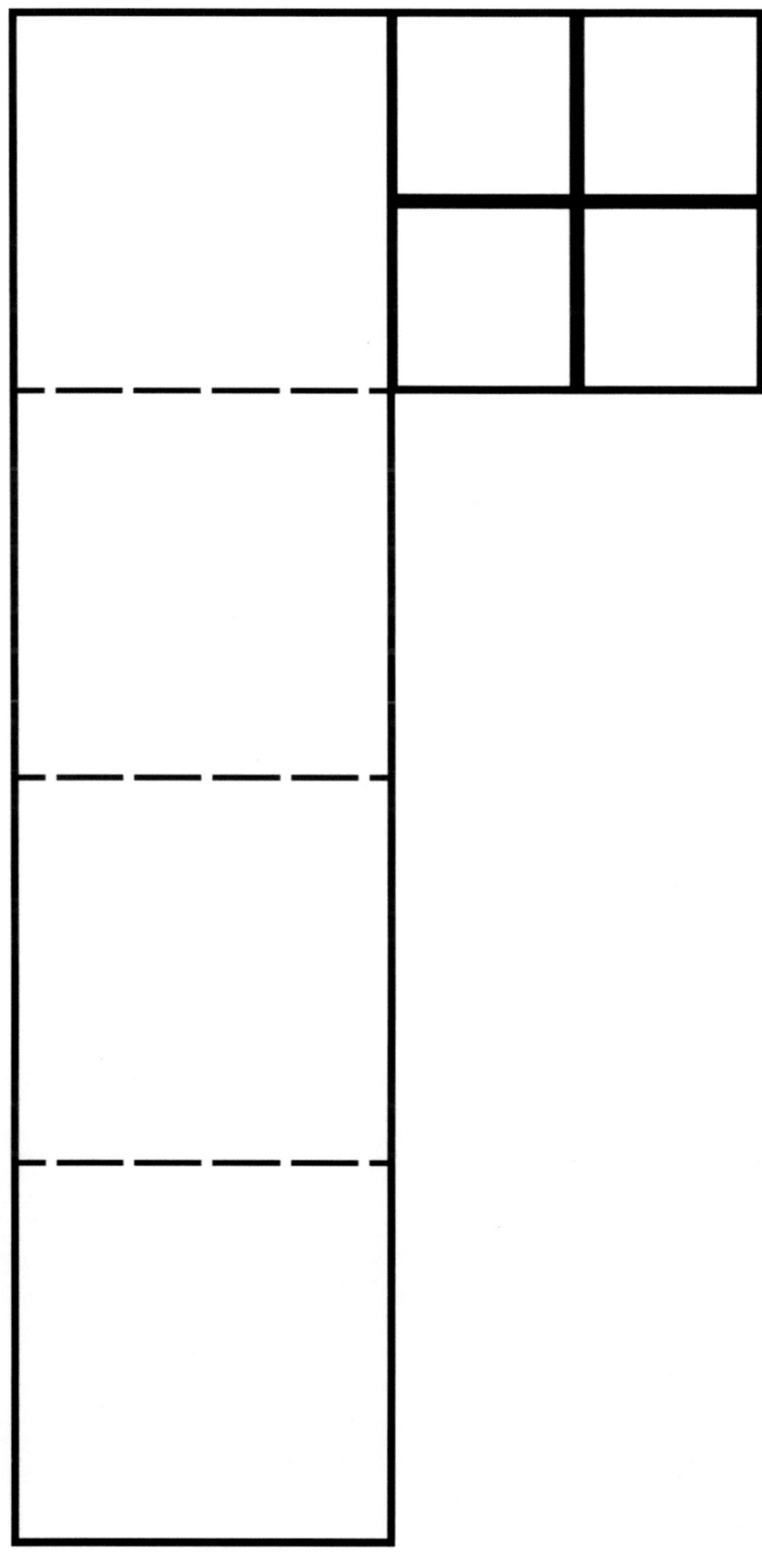

Appendix E (1 of 2)

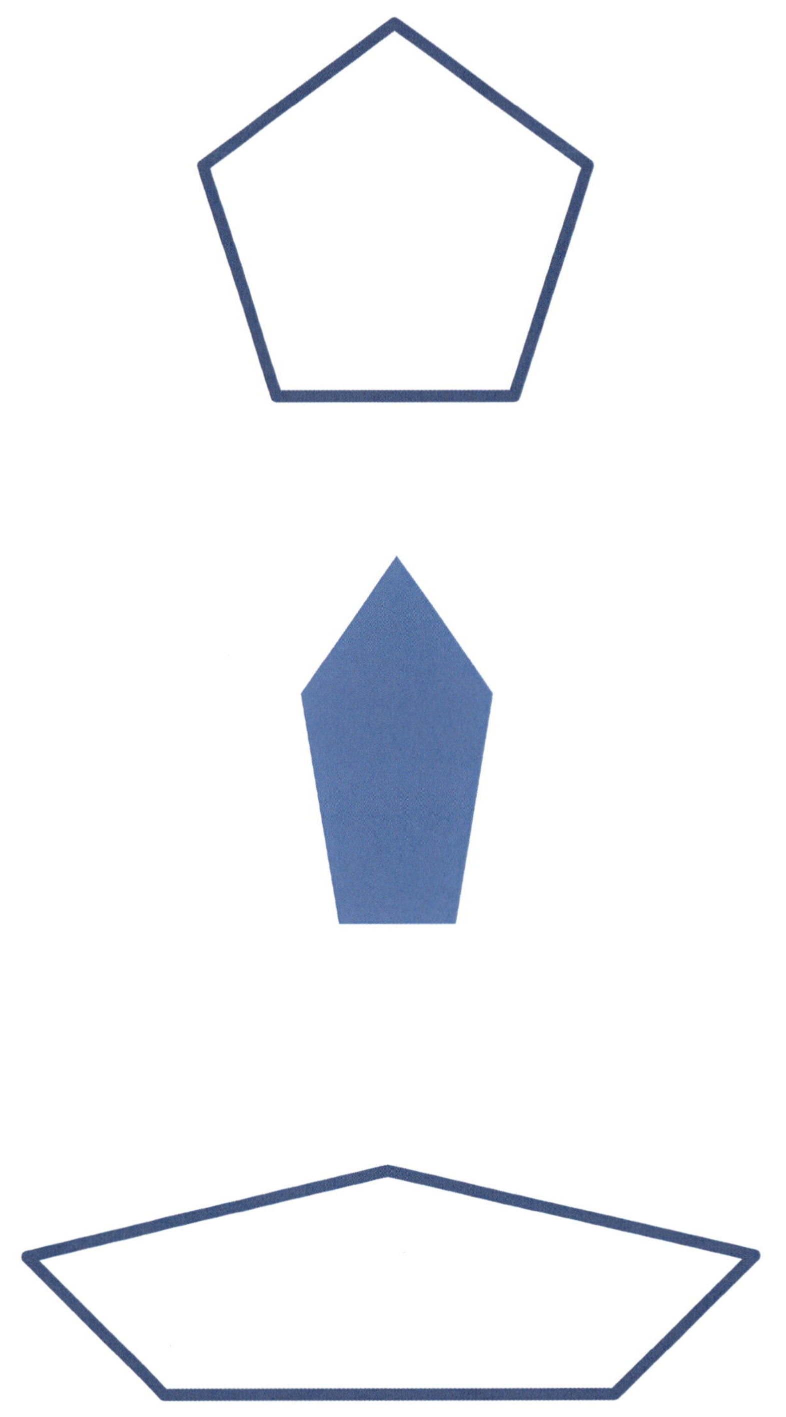

Appendix E (2 of 2)

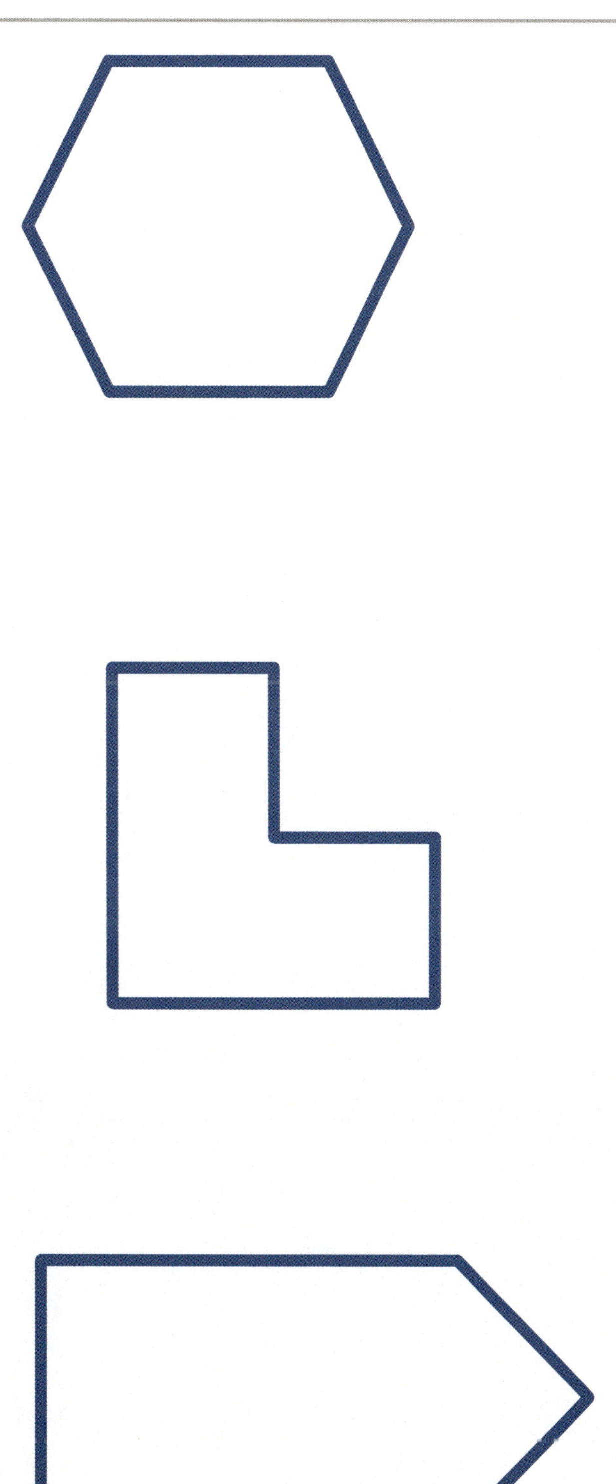

Appendix F (4 Patios)

Made in the USA
Monee, IL
14 June 2023